# Constructivist Psychotherapy

T0332365

Constructivist psychotherapy focuses on the meaning that clients attribute to their world, and the way that this shapes their life and contributes to their difficulties. In this book, Robert A. Neimeyer, a leading figure in the field, provides a clear and accessible explanation of the key features of this approach.

*Constructivist Psychotherapy: Distinctive Features* concentrates on the 30 key commitments that distinguish constructivism from other cognitive behavioral perspectives. Divided into two parts—Theory and Practice—this straightforward book is illustrated throughout with case material and recent research findings.

Neimeyer provides us with a fresh perspective on familiar material, together with a clear, concise introduction to material that the reader may be less familiar with, making this book a valuable text for professionals in training as well as a source of new ideas for practising therapists of constructivist psychotherapy.

**Robert A. Neimeyer** is a professor in the Department of Psychology at the University of Memphis and the editor of the *Journal of Constructivist Psychology*. He also maintains an active private practice in Memphis, Tennessee.

Cognitive behavioural therapy (CBT) occupies a central position in the move towards evidence-based practice and is frequently used in the clinical environment. Yet there is no one universal approach to CBT and clinicians speak of first-, second-, and even third-wave approaches.

This series provides straightforward, accessible guides to a number of CBT methods, clarifying the distinctive features of each approach. The series editor, Windy Dryden, successfully brings together experts from each discipline to summarise the 30 main aspects of their approach divided into theoretical and practical features.

*The CBT Distinctive Features Series* will be essential reading for psychotherapists, counsellors, and psychologists of all orientations who want to learn more about the range of new and developing cognitive-behavioural approaches.

**Titles in the series:**

For further information about this series please visit:
www.routledgementalhealth.com/cbt-distinctive-features

# Constructivist Psychotherapy

## Distinctive Features

## Robert A. Neimeyer

Routledge
Taylor & Francis Group

LONDON AND NEW YORK

First published 2009 by Routledge
2 Park Square, Milton Park, Abingdon, Oxon OX14 4RN

Simultaneously published in the USA and Canada
by Routledge
711 Third Avenue, New York, NY 10017

*Routledge is an imprint of the Taylor & Francis Group, an Informa business*

Typeset in Times by Garfield Morgan,
Swansea, West Glamorgan
Cover design by Sandra Heath

*British Library Cataloguing in Publication Data*
A catalogue record for this book is available from the British Library

*Library of Congress Cataloging-in-Publication Data*
Neimeyer, Robert A., 1954–
   Constructivist psychotherapy : distinctive features / Robert A.
Neimeyer.
      p. ; cm.
   Includes bibliographical references and index.
   ISBN 978-0-415-44233-6 (hardback) – ISBN 978-0-415-44234-3
(pbk.) 1. Personal construct therapy. 2. Constructivism (Psychology)
I. Title.
   [DNLM: 1. Psychotherapy–methods. 2. Personal Construct Theory.
WM 420 N414c 2009]
   RC489.P46N45 2009
   616.89'14–dc22

                                                         2008033868

ISBN: 978-0-415-44233-6 (hbk)
ISBN: 978-0-415-44234-3 (pbk)

# Contents

# Introduction

Being asked to write a book about the distinctive features of constructivist psychotherapy (CPT) represents simultaneously a blessing and a curse. On the one hand, being given generous space to unpack the practice of this exciting postmodern perspective is a gift: freed of the constraints of a chapter-length summary with its often mandated structure, I've been given the opportunity to say what matters to me about constructivism, and why it has been a good companion in my work as a psychotherapist for the past 30 years. On the other hand, how do I put into words the deeply personal ways that this philosophical position has percolated into my practice with so many people, or informed my own thinking, much less that of the colorful cast of characters who would confess a loose or passionate allegiance to this clinical tradition?

My attempt to meet this challenge has been guided by four criteria. First, I have attempted to write simply. My goal in these pages was to demystify a perspective that is sometimes rightly regarded as philosophically abstruse and procedurally obscure, as I believe in my bones that it is neither. In doing so I should warn the reader that this is not intended as a book for "insiders"; those looking for densely epistemological treatises on constructivist philosophy, fascinating though it may be, will simply need to look elsewhere. Instead, I have written the book for those I train in dozens of workshops, conferences and lecture halls each year, the majority of whom are relative newcomers to the approach. I hope they find it approachable!

Second, I have focused on constructivism's distinctive features. This, of course, was the basic charge of the series editor, Windy Dryden, who requested that I concentrate on 30 key commitments of constructivism that distinguish it from the panoply of cognitive behavioral perspectives with which it is sometimes grouped. Fortunately, this is an easy task, as the postmodern pastiche in which constructivists participate is richly variegated, spanning horizons that range from the deeply personal to the broadly social, and which differ fundamentally from the central tendencies of their cognitive colleagues from other traditions.

Third, I have written from the heart as well as the head. The holistic quality of constructivist therapy, with its strong emphasis on emotion as well as meaning and action, supports my decision to acknowledge in these pages my personal predilections as well as to speak as a constructivist scholar. This further implies that the principles and procedures I describe and illustrate are inevitably those that speak to me, and I concede at the outset that another constructivist might well have written a very different primer of his or her practice. This is in itself in keeping with the individuality of the perspective, although I hope this book will also serve as a doorway for the interested reader to pass through on the way to exploring the work of others.

Fourth, I have tried to ground abstract principles in concrete practices. Throughout the book, literally from the first page through the last, the reader will meet many of those who have shared their life struggles and successes with me in the intimate partnership we call psychotherapy. I hope their stories, edited with appropriate concern for their confidentiality, help make the realm of constructivist ideas come alive for the practitioner or student who wonders what these precepts look like when the "rubber meets the road" of clinical practice.

Although I accept full responsibility for the rendition of constructivism offered here, in another sense this book is necessarily a work written by many hands. Far from viewing the "construction of reality" as a project undertaken by an isolated subjectivity, constructivism sees meaning making as relational, social and cultural to the core. Likewise, constructivism itself has been shaped by the discourses of a diverse global community of scholars, scientists and practitioners, many of whom I have had the privilege to call friends. Among the very many others whose voices speak through me in these pages are my colleagues Bruce Ecker, Ken Gergen, David Epston, Hubert Hermans, David Winter, Heidi Levitt, Ze'ev Frankel, Les Greenberg, Art Bohart, Larry Leitner, Jon Raskin, Sara Bridges, Guillem Feixas, Harry Procter, Laura Brown, my brother, Greg Neimeyer, and perhaps even the ghost of George Kelly! Nor am I indebted only to peers and predecessors, as the work of protégées also finds expression in what follows, and most especially that of my young colleagues Joe Currier, Jason Holland, James Gillies and Jessica van Dyke, the last of whom tirelessly perused the manuscript for errors subtle enough to confound even the spelling and grammar-checking programs of Microsoft® Word.

And finally, I feel a special obligation to acknowledge the implicit contribution to this book and the larger narrative of my life made by three colleagues, Vittorio Guidano, Michael Mahoney and Michael White whose untimely deaths in 1999, 2006 and 2008, respectively, deprived constructivism of three of its most memorable and influential leaders. It seems fitting, then, to close with a poem of my own that honors the memory of these three colleagues, whose voices continue to echo in the halls of a theoretical edifice they did so much to build. The field was made richer by their presence in it.

Robert A. Neimeyer
*Memphis, TN, USA, June 2008*

### *Room*

Even the chair defines you
by your absence.
It lifts its arms
to embrace yours, opens its lap
to cup your form in its soft shape.
Without you,
it is an empty hand.

On the footstool the books
mill in their randomness,
forget their call to common purpose.
The pens on your desk
have bled dry of words.
Your tablet is a tombstone
without inscription.

This is how we are cast
by the long light of your shadow,
persist in our objective irrelevance.
Collectively, we have lost
the threads of memory,
of intention, dropped the beads
from time's limp string.
The clock's pulse
measures the silence
like a tin heart, registers
only hours *since*, never *until*.

Slowly we are hollowing
ourselves through our grief,
as rocks are carved by sand
in a hard wind.
When we have let go of enough
of what we were

and grow perfect in our nothingness,
we will at last find an end
to the yearning,
and finally

have room for you.

# An illustrative therapy

Joanne W's pursuit of therapy was prompted by a number of recent but frightening physical symptoms, which included dizziness, rapid heartbeat, and racing pulse, accompanied by seemingly inexplicable spirals of "nervousness." When thorough medical testing disclosed no organic basis for these reactions, she was referred for psychotherapy with a diagnosis of "panic attacks of psychogenic origin," although Joanne herself was hard put to explain the reasons for her paralyzing anxiety in terms that were convincing to her or to others. Presenting for her first session attractively attired in a conservative, but well-tailored suit, Joanne noted that her symptoms first appeared when she prepared to leave the eastern city that had been "her only home" some five months earlier to follow her husband's "call" to take a position as the pastor of a southern African-American church over a thousand miles away. Now, distant from her mother, sisters, and friends in the community that had shaped and sustained her, she found herself becoming increasingly reclusive lest members of the new congregation discover her "emotional problems" and label her as "crazy." Over the past several weeks, Joanne confided, she had even begun to "pull away" from her husband, George, and 12-year-old daughter, Leitha, deepening her concern that she not only was failing as the "first lady" of her church, but also was "losing herself" and those she loved.

After spending a few minutes exploring Joanne's understanding of her problem in more detail, I inquired about any previous experiences she might have had with therapy, as a way of seeking her consultation on what therapeutic styles or methods had worked especially well—or poorly—for her. Joanne responded that her only previous exposure to therapy had been in the context of her "spiritual formation" counseling a few years before, part of which focused on her psychological issues and needs. The major issue at the time, she recalled in a controlled fashion, had been her father's death 6 years ago, the stress of which had been compounded by the long illness that preceded it and for which she and her mother had been the primary caregivers. Tears rolled down Joanne's cheeks in response to my empathic inquiry about the trembling in her lip as she recounted her father's passing, and she noted that she had only in the past year begun to cry for him, as his uncharacteristic "meanness" during his illness left her more with a sense of numbness and relief than grief over his passing. Now, she realized, she truly missed him, and speaking quietly but unevenly through the haze of tears, added that, "He would have been able to give me advice about moving, if only he were here."

Alerted to the emotional vividness of this material for Joanne some six years after her father's death, and struck by her spontaneous linkage of his absence with the problems in her relocation that had precipitated the anxiety attacks, I gently asked Joanne if she would like to invite her father to join us in the therapy room, to reopen a relationship with her that had been interrupted by his illness and death. Intrigued, she accepted the suggestion, and with my guidance, began a conversation with her father, who we symbolically offered an empty chair positioned across from his daughter. Sobbing, Joanne recounted to her father the outlines of her current problems, and, after a few seconds of silence, deepened her disclosure to include her feeling of guilt for having "abandoned" him by leaving the city in which he had lived for his whole adult life, to return to the South he had known only as a boy.

Accepting my suggestion that she take her father's place and respond to what she had said, Joanne changed chairs, dried her tears, and offered reassurance, concluding with, "Don't worry, baby, I'll come visit you," words that rung strangely hollow in view of the poignant sense of loss Joanne had shared only moments before. Again taking her own seat at my gesture, Joanne repeated the words I tentatively offered to her: "You can't visit me, dad. You're dead." Joanne then poured forth both her grief and self-doubt, punctuated by wracking sobs. As she grew quiet, I again invited her into her father's chair, where, unprompted, she provided loving and genuine reassurance, affirming that, despite his death, he would always be with her, always believe in her. This interaction triggered a startling insight for Joanne. In her words, "I realize now that I *can* keep him, that he *can* be with me, and that I can even come to know him more through the South that he loved." Buoyed up by the newfound reconnection with her father, Joanne then went on to place her own sense of uprootedness and disloyalty in the context of her relationship with the surviving members of her family of origin, who, like her, were "struggling together to make sense of this new transition." As the first session neared its end, Joanne somewhat sheepishly shared her wish to pursue an advanced university degree despite her "first lady" status, but serving as a cultural interpreter, described for the benefit of her Caucasian therapist the implicit social expectations that constrained this potentially "selfish" goal within her African-American faith community. Eager to pursue the "fresh ideas" generated in the session, Joanne closed by requesting another appointment.

In her remaining three bi-weekly sessions, Joanne deepened her exploration of both her history of loss, revisiting the death of an infant son early in her marriage, and her renewed effort to "find her voice" as a woman in her own right in her family and church community. As she did so, she remarked with some surprise that life was starting to seem somehow "more real," and she related with pride several concrete instances in which she had negotiated important family decisions with her husband, played a more active role in providing guidance to her pre-teen daughter, and "stood up" for innovative programs she believed in in the church. In all of this, she continued to feel a strong sense of her father's presence and his pride in her and the feeling that something had "lifted" for her in the pivotal "conversation" with him in the opening session. In Joanne's own words, she no longer felt "held back" and was gratified by George's support for her being her own "outspoken" self, even to the point of wearing casual clothes to both church committee meetings and therapy sessions. Perhaps most remarkably, she had been entirely freed of the panic symptoms from the point of her "conversation" with her father onward, despite these symptoms never having been made the specific targets of thera-peutic intervention. Therapy concluded by reflecting on the "changed narrative" of Joanne's life, which re-established a sense of continuity with who she had been (as anchored in an ongoing relationship with her supportive father), while also permitting her to "re-author" aspects of her identity in critical living relationships. Follow-up indicated that these changes were further consolidated over the months that followed.

As suggested by this opening case vignette, constructivist psychotherapy (CPT) draws on several therapeutic traditions—in this case particularly the humanistic, systemic, and feminist—while also reinterpreting and extending these tradi-tions in light of characteristically postmodern themes, having to do especially with the primacy of personal meaning, the con-struction of identity in a social field, and the revision of life narratives that are incoherent or restrictive. Although the variety of postmodern approaches frustrates any attempt to offer a single definition of their features, in general they tend to be more collaborative than authoritative, more developmental than symptom-oriented, more process-directive than content-focused, and more reflective than psychoeducational. My goal in this brief book is to demystify many of the concepts and practices associated with this confederation of contemporary approaches, providing a foothold in the sometimes-daunting postmodern terrain for those students and professionals intrepid enough to explore it. We will begin by considering the intellectual and historical backdrop that informs constructivism and that helps shape its distinctive approaches to the conceptualization and treatment of psychosocial problems.

# Part 1

# THE DISTINCTIVE THEORETICAL FEATURES OF CPT

No intellectual development arrives on the scene as a result of the "immaculate conception" of its founder. Instead, each inevitably arises from the commingling of concepts from previous generations, representing the fertile marriage of ideas having different intellectual pedigrees. Extending this "marriage" metaphor, we might even say that every nascent theory represents "something old, something new, something borrowed, and something 'true'"—at least to its adherents! In other words, every emerging perspective repackages the wisdom of earlier thinkers, adds its own insights and innovations, draws on other streams of thought (with or without crediting the source), and then propounds this complex mixture as in some sense a valid reflection of "reality"—at least within the constraints imposed by the limits of present knowledge. Of course, whether this distinctive amalgam of concepts and practices strikes other people as intriguing, insulting or incomprehensible will depend in turn on their own personal theories and philosophies—just as constructivists would argue! I'll therefore start with some of the distinctive assumptions that constructivist psychotherapists share, and move from there to the practices they inspire.

1

## Constructing a world

Newcomers to postmodern therapies are typically of two types: those who are closet philosophers and share a fascination with theory, and students of a more practical bent who are frustrated with this same tendency toward abstraction! My goal here is to provide just enough orientation to the philosophic frameworks that support constructivist practice to highlight its distinctiveness, taking care to ground some of the loftier concepts in concrete clinical illustrations and methods. Thus, if I sometimes simplify the daunting complexity of postmodern discourse, I hope I can be forgiven. Fortunately, high-level discussions of the theoretical underpinnings of the therapies discussed here are in good supply, and I will point toward some of these throughout the discussion for those readers who want to delve more deeply into the concepts behind the clinical practice.

If there is a unifying theme that links postmodern forms of psychotherapy, it is at the level of their *epistemology*, or theory of knowledge. Although most therapists who work within this perspective acknowledge that a "real world" exists outside of human consciousness or language, they are much more interested in the nuances in people's construction of the world than they are in evaluating the extent to which such constructions are "true" in representing a presumably external reality. This emphasis on the active, form-giving nature of the mind dates back at least to the Italian historian Giambattista Vico (1668–1744), who traced the development of thought to the attempt to understand the world by projecting upon it human motives, myths, fables, and linguistic abstractions. The German philosopher Immanuel Kant (1724–1804) likewise emphasized the transformative character of the mind, which necessarily imposes spatial, temporal, and causal order on the phenomena of experience. From these philosophers, constructivists borrowed a model of knowledge as an active structuring of experience, rather than a passive or receptive assimilation of "things in themselves," uncontaminated by human knowing.

2

# The function of fiction

At the threshold to the twentieth century, these themes were elaborated by the German analytic philosopher, Hans Vaihinger (1852–1933), whose *Philosophy of "As If"* asserted that people develop "workable fictions" (e.g., of mathematical infinity or God) to order and transcend the hard data of experience, and establish distinctively human goals (Vaihinger, 1924). A similar emphasis on the distinction between our linguistic "map" of experience and the "territory" of the world was made by the Polish intellectual Alfred Korzybski (1879–1950), whose system of general semantics focused on the role of the speaker in assigning meanings to events. From these thinkers, constructivists drew the implication that human beings operate on the basis of symbolic linguistic constructs that help them navigate in the world without contacting it in any simple, direct way. Stated differently, proponents of postmodernism argue that people live in an interpreted world, one organized as much by their individual and collective categories of meaning as by the structure of an "objective" world of external stimuli. In clinical practice, this carries the implication that therapy is more a matter of *intervening in meaning* than it is a procedure for ameliorating unwanted symptoms or training people in more adequate coping skills, as illustrated in the vignette of Joanne with which this book opened.

3

# Personal knowledge

By the 1930s, these and parallel philosophical influences began to find expression in psychology, inspiring a focus on the ways in which people actively *construct* experience, rather than simply "register" environmental stimuli in a *tabula rasa* fashion. Among the psychologists to take this avowedly "constructivist" turn were the Swiss developmental psychologist, Jean Piaget, who traced the qualitative transformations through which children schematized the physical and social world, and the British experimental psychologist, Fredric Bartlett, who demonstrated that memories did not simply entail recalling stored events, but instead were constructed in light of present motives through the guidance of mental *schemas*. Both influences continue to be felt in contemporary research on autobiographical memory, which examines the construction and periodic consolidation of a shifting sense of identity throughout adult life (Fireman, McVay, & Flanagan, 2003; Neisser & Fivush, 1994).

The first person to develop a thoroughgoing theory of psychotherapy that drew upon these philosophic ideas was the American clinical psychologist, George Kelly. Working in the relative isolation of rural Kansas in the 1930s and 1940s, Kelly confronted the overwhelming psychological needs of farming communities that had been devastated by the twin crises of the Dust Bowl and the Great Depression (R. A. Neimeyer, 1999). This prompted Kelly to design efficient psychotherapeutic procedures in which clients were coached to enact carefully constructed fictional identities in their daily lives for a fixed period of time (usually only 2 or 3 weeks), as a way of helping people free themselves from the press of circumstances and experiment with quite different ways of living. Kelly's *fixed-role therapy* was therefore the first form of brief therapy, and fore-shadowed the use of dramatic and narrative strategies of change incorporated in many contemporary constructivist therapies. Eventually, Kelly (1955/1991) drafted a comprehensive *psychology of personal constructs* that placed these procedures in a rigorous theoretical context and suggested diagnostic, therapeutic, and research methods targeting the unique personal construct systems that individuals devised to structure and anticipate the themes of their lives.

A foundational principle of Kelly's perspective was that each person has a one-of-a-kind operating system—or *personal construct system* in his terms—that provides an idiosyncratic "map" of the world and one's place within it. Far from being a regrettable form of idiosyncrasy to be rectified by "right thinking," the elimination of "cognitive errors" or the clarification of personal "distortions," the individualism and diversity in our outlooks were for Kelly quintessentially human, the source of both our strengths as a species and our inherent frustrations. That is, the tendency of every single human being to construct a personal theory that imputes different meanings to (partially) shared events contributes to the richness and diversity of relational, social, and cultural life, just as it also poses real puzzles in attempting to "step into" and "indwell" the sometimes subtly or surprisingly alien perspectives of "the other." An example of the latter arose in my recent telephone contact with a young man in suicidal crisis. After an intensive hour of my attempting to empathize with his pain following his partner's decision to leave him, and to respond constructively to his self-blame and hopelessness about the ending of the relationship, he paused and said in a hushed tone, "You sound like my *best friend*." For a moment I felt touched and took heart, hoping I had at least constructed enough of a bridge between us that a follow-up face-to-face session would be helpful. Within a minute, however, I came to understand that for him this phrase meant, "You sound just like my best friend, because you both talk in an emotionally controlled tone about anguishing events that are tearing me apart, and so I can't trust either of you to really understand or help!" Grasping this idio-syncratic meaning, I backed up and started again, acknowl-edging my position as a concerned outsider, but offering the active, structuring steps I could to help him through the crisis. Much of the purpose of constructivist assessment methods, as described below, is to help reveal the meanings behind the words, the deeper themes between the lines of the stories clients tell themselves and us about what brings them to therapy.

4

## Living on the frontier

In lieu of a fundamental motivational principle to explain why people do the things they do, Kelly proposed that human beings are basically "forms of motion" who don't need to be pushed and pulled by internal needs or external stimuli in order to "emit behavior." Instead, he proposed that people are intrinsically active, and our goal as psychologists is to understand not *why* they act in the first place, but rather *in what direction* their activity is likely to carry them. For him, the answers were to be found in the network of personal constructs or meanings through which people anticipate the world, and most especially the actions and reactions of other people. This quest to construct and validate a set of reference axes in order to chart action in the social world and to organize one's own actions and commitments in it was for him never ending; we spend a lifetime looking for recurrent themes in events, using them to predict what will happen next, investing our time, effort, resources, and ultimately our lives in varying degrees in these, encountering the relevant events, suffering the invalidation of our hypotheses or celebrating their usefulness, and actively experimenting with revised or deepened convictions as a result. But for better or worse, we never arrive in a "cognitive Eden" in which we are forever secure, and where the terrain and rules of the game are stable and familiar. Instead, our forward movement toward an uncertain future is like living on the frontier, confronting challenges and innovating solutions as we move forward, pushing back the boundaries of the known world. In fact, accepting the inevitable anxiety of facing continual novelty can be far healthier, Kelly suggested, than falling back repeatedly on old constructs that may be well worn, but stultifying, in essence "choosing" to live with familiar frustrations rather than jettison previous patterns and face the discomforts of reinventing ourselves and our worlds.

Consider the experience of one of my current clients, Melanie, a woman in her early forties whose experience with an "entitled," materialistic mother and "workaholic" (and alcoholic) father in her childhood and teen years left her yearning for a kind of personal care and attention that was in short supply in her home. Not surprisingly, she found herself adopting the family construct of "bucking up" like her father, displaying an uncomplaining work ethic, against the backdrop of the anticipation that other people would simply be selfish and demanding if she permitted them to draw close to her. Although this role vis-à-vis others served her well in educational and career realms, it was far less successful in her relational world, as her efficiency and task focus made it hard for others to connect with her, except in a businesslike way. Finally, lonely and sad at forty, she allowed herself to "slow down" with Brian, who manifested the sort of casual orientation toward the world of work that she envied and who showed the ability to care for her that she craved. They fell in love, and she soon gave birth to a child. This hoped-for development, however, precipitated an unexpected crisis, as Melanie's urge to reduce her hours at a demanding job to spend more time with her baby raised the specter of significantly reduced income, with no corresponding eagerness on Brian's part to seek a more high-powered position for himself in order to compensate. This situation strongly invalidated Melanie's anticipations of the new family life she was "entitled" to—an idyllic and protected sphere in which she and her child could enjoy the generous time together she never had as a child—and not surprisingly threw her back upon her old and ingrained family construct to navigate the experience: she, like her father, needed to "buck up" once again and silently but resentfully accommodate to the role of primary breadwinner. Motivated to seek therapy by the fear that she was "becoming her father," she soon recognized that she was caught as much in a construct system that limited her range of alternatives as she was in external exigencies. Our work now consists of understanding the deep purposes served by her current position—including maintaining loyalty to her family of origin, preserving her sense of being "deserving" of something she never had, and more—and reaching for alternative constructs that will help her anticipate and move toward a family life that is something other than the mirror image of her parents.

5

# Redefining reality

Although interest in personal construct theory grew slowly in the decades that followed the publication of his work, Kelly was in a sense ahead of his time. Certainly, an emphasis on the role of personal systems of meaning and the fictional construction of identities seemed an odd fit in a field dominated by a concern with unconscious motives on the one hand and the modification of observable behavior on the other. Consequently, it was not until a postmodern *Zeitgeist* began to work its way into the human sciences and the helping professions some 30–40 years later that significant numbers of psychotherapy theorists began to rediscover Kelly's insights and extend them in radically new directions.

What is *postmodernism* (PM), and what is its relevance for clinical practice? As the term suggests, "posties" can best be defined in relation to the traditional intellectual framework that they strive to succeed, undermine, or critique, namely, *modernism*. Modernism is a broad concept, almost too broad to define with any precision, because it encompasses so many domains of social life. However, as applied to the human sciences, modernism embodies the Enlightenment faith in technological and human progress through accumulation of legitimate knowledge. Throughout its century-long history, psychology has for the most part followed this paradigm through the development of logical, experimental, and statistical methods presumed to yield objective data, providing a secure foundation for theories that were assumed to reflect, with as little distortion as possible, the universal and timeless "realities" of human behavior. "Truth," in this view, is discovered a bit at a time, whether the "truth" concerned general laws of human behavior or concrete historical determinants of that behavior in the lives of individuals in psychotherapy. At the core of this program was the belief in a knowable world, and with it, a knowable self. In large part, it is this modernist faith in logic, science, and objectivity that underpins traditional cognitive therapies, with their emphasis on critiquing irrational or distorted patterns of thinking that presumably maintain problematic emotions and behaviors. Therapy, in this view, becomes the systematic application of techniques to foster cognitive restructuring so as to promote improved "reality contact," and with it, better adjustment (R. A. Neimeyer, 1995b).

Dissenting from this traditional view, postmodernism calls into question the very concept of timeless certainty, asserting that all human "realities" are necessarily personal, cultural, and linguistic constructs—although they are no less substantial or important for this reason (Appignanesi & Garratt, 1995). "Truth," in this view, is actually constituted by individuals and social groups and reflects the dominant social ideologies of the day, however fallible these turn out to be in the hindsight of later generations. For example, cultural norms about the appropriate roles of women or ethnic minorities, laws that prohibit and punish certain behavior, and even psychiatric diagnoses are all historically situated (and changing) social constructions, but this does not mitigate their impact on those subjected to them. Scholars working from a PM perspective therefore seek to reveal the often hidden ways in which reality and power are constructed in the course of social life (Derrida, 1978; Foucault, 1970), and therapists and activists animated by this view attempt to analyze and "deconstruct" these same patterns when they function to limit or constrain the possibilities for a given person or community.

6

# Living in language

A corollary of this shift from realism to relativism is that as the apparent power of objective circumstances grows weaker, the power of language, broadly defined to include all symbolic means of labeling reality and regulating human behavior, grows stronger. In this view language is not simply a way of *representing* reality, it is a way of *creating* it, literally bringing new social realities into being in the terms that are used, whether in a casual conversation between two friends who agree that a co-worker is a "bitch" or in cultural discourses that define "beauty" in terms that require the relentless pursuit of thinness. Constructivists and their close cousins, the social constructionists (Gergen, 1999), therefore grow interested in how people use language in a way that shapes and delimits how people appraise themselves, others (especially vulnerable others), and life difficulties in ways that are problematic and disempowering. A spirit of "resistance" against the taken-for-granted assumptions of cultural "texts" in the service of personal or social transformation is especially evident in some PM approaches, like the narrative therapies to be discussed later.

Rather than elaborate further at this point on the implications of constructivist epistemology for postmodern practice, we will revisit these themes in the points that follow, considering some of their concrete expressions in the conceptualization of the self, psychopathology, psychological assessment, and therapeutic practice.

7

# Deconstructing the self

The concept of "personality" is a two-edged sword. At one level, it serves a useful integrative function, helping explain how the myriad forms and facets of human functioning are organized into a larger and potentially more holistic pattern. Personality, in this sense, is what makes you *you*, a self both distinguishable from others and recognizable, with meaningful variations and developments, across time. As such, the personality or "self" has played a central role in the history of psychotherapy, serving as an orienting concept for clinical diagnosis, as well as a target for clinical interventions. From Freud's classic structural formulation of ego functioning (Freud, 1940/1964) to its elaboration by object relations (Kernberg, 1976) and self-theorists (Kohut, 1971), and from early conceptions of the "proprium" (Allport, 1961) to humanistic theories of self-development (Rogers, 1961), various models of personality have provided a foundation for theories of psychotherapy. Even scientifically parsimonious cognitive-behavioral therapies (Beck, 1993) implicitly presume a foundational role for the self in their focus on training clients in self-monitoring, recording of self-talk, and similar procedures. Viewed in a critical sociohistorical perspective, such models can be seen as expressing a modernist discourse in which the self is viewed as individualistic, singular, essential, stable, and knowable, at least in principle (R. A. Neimeyer, 1998). It follows that psychotherapy, as a series of authoritative technical procedures to bring about self-change, would focus chiefly on intrapsychic disorders that impair adaptation and then treat them in such a way as to enhance the client's self-actualization, self-control, self-efficacy, and the like.

In a sense, postmodern approaches to psychotherapy both extend and problematize this conception of selfhood. On the one hand, the self retains its role as an organizing concept in many constructivist theories, which focus on the "core ordering processes" (Mahoney, 1991) by which individuals construct a sense of personal identity in an intersubjective field (Guidano, 1991). Moreover, in keeping with humanistic personality theories, constructivists typically emphasize the role of personal meanings in shaping people's responses to events and regard human beings as capable of at least a bounded agency in determining the course of their lives (Kelly, 1955/1991). In this view, we *are* our constructs: personality can be seen as the composite of our myriad ways of interpreting, anticipating, and responding to the social world. For example, early abusive experiences in intimate relationships might have made it compellingly important for a female client to discriminate between *people who are safe to be close to* and *those who are dangerous*. Once this "personal construct" is integrated into her system, however, it says as much about her as it does about her world, as she vigilantly screens possible relational partners in terms of the safety or danger that they represent, and behaves toward them accordingly. Ultimately, Kelly argued that some constructs become "superordinate" or central to our systems of living, creating hierarchical matrices of meaning that scaffold our interactions with others. Viewed from this perspective, the "self" is not constituted by any set of inherent, essential inner qualities or traits, but instead simply represents the distillation of our shifting efforts to engage the social world.

On the other hand, some postmodern theorists regard even this conception of personality as suspiciously romantic, expressing the cognitivism and individualism of Western culture, with its emphasis on "well-integrated" and sovereign selves as the hallmark of personal identity. In this more radical and critical vision, identity is far less stable and coherent, at best comprising a "dialogical self" whose distinguishable parts vie for voice in our inner world (Hermans & Dimaggio, 2004), and in its more extreme forms herald the "death of the self" altogether (Lather, 1992). Considering personality as simply a linguistic construction, a view of the "saturated self" as populated by the contradictory discourses in which one is immersed threatens the very conception of the individual as a coherent entity with identifiable boundaries and properties (Gergen, 1991). Thus, in this version of social constructionism, it is little wonder that we as individuals are fraught with uncertainty, conflict and contradiction, insofar as our individual lives are merely the sites of incompatible discourses of identity (e.g., about the requirements for being a good partner, parent or professional, all anchored in diverse conversations and media images), each of which "positions" us as a certain kind of person, but in ways that typically make competing demands of us (Efran & Cook, 2000). Such a perspective further tempers the traditional, modernist assumption of the ultimate knowability of the self and, with it, the relevance of rationalistic self-analysis and self-control procedures (R. A. Neimeyer, 1993a, 1995b). Instead, it follows from this more socialized view of selfhood that psycho-therapeutic procedures for fostering change would need to tack between the self and social system, helping clients articulate, elaborate, and negotiate those (inter)personal meanings by which they organize their experience and action, as well as the sometimes oppressive or conflictual role of cultural discourses that "colonize" their lives (R. A. Neimeyer, 1995a). This attention to the processes by which identity is constructed and maintained in a social field is evident in family and systemic expressions of postmodern therapies that will be covered below.

## Systems within systems: The epigenetic model

Placed in a larger perspective, these relative emphases on the personal versus social construction of identity can be seen as expressions of a broader "epigenetic systems" model (see Figure 1) that views human meaning and action as the emergent outcome of a series of hierarchically embedded systems and subsystems (Mascolo, Craig-Bray, & Neimeyer, 1997). In biology, epigenesis stands in contrast to theories that view an organism's structures, behaviors, or capacities as either essential and inborn or as the simple and predictable result of maturational unfolding. Instead, new structures are seen as emerging through the interaction of a multi-leveled organism–environment system, in which the functioning of each constituent feature (e.g., chromosomes) is shaped through transactions of more basic levels (e.g., genes) and higher-order ones (e.g., cell matrices). As applied to human functioning, epigenesis implies that meaning and action emerge from a similarly multi-layered system of systems, which include bio-genetic, personal-agentic, dyadic-relational, and cultural-linguistic levels. *Bio-genetic* systems refer to all systems below the level of the organism-as-agent (genetic, cellular, and organ systems). The *personal-agentic* level refers to functioning of the organism as a personality, having a bounded degree of choice in determining its own development. *Dyadic-relational* systems emerge out of co-actions between two or more individuals (e.g., family systems), which are further nested within larger *cultural-linguistic* systems of cultural patterns, institutions, discourses, and beliefs.

In this integrative model, all psychologically significant structures and symptoms emerge from the complex interaction

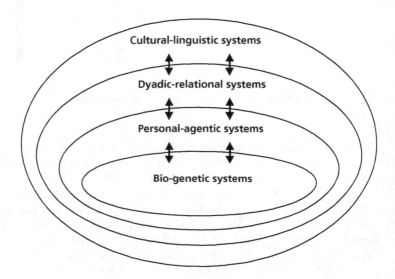

**Figure 1** The epigenetic model of the organism–environment system

of all levels of this comprehensive system, rather than from a given level considered in isolation. For example, a young man's experience of depression can best be understood not simply as an expression of a bio-genetic predisposition to mood disorder, but also as an experience that compels exploration of its significance for his developing personality (or sense of inner division), his relationships (particularly with his family, peers, and employer), and cultural scripts or narratives (especially those concerned with what it means to be a "man" and dominant and perhaps oppressive discourses of "mental illness").

Although many different processes and structures might be studied within this broad epigenetic approach, several constructivist and postmodern psychologies converge in taking as their unit of analysis the *situated interpretive activity* of individuals and groups (Mascolo et al., 1997). This carries four specific implications that have relevance for psychotherapy. First, the concept of *interpretation* suggests that all psychological and social activity involves assessments of the meaning that events have for people, in keeping with the core emphases of constructivism (R. A. Neimeyer & Mahoney, 1995). Second, the focus on interpretive *activity* suggests that action is primary, whether expressed mainly on behavioral or symbolic levels; "construing" no less than "doing" is a way of *accomplishing something* in the world, not merely thinking about it. Third, the emphasis on *situated* interpretive activity implies that human activity always emerges in a context, which typically involves other people or has been structured by previous social or linguistic activity. Human functioning always requires coordinating with the demands of this larger social context, as this evolves across the life span and across history. And, finally, the emphasis on the situated character of activity suggests that individuals are not naturally unified beings, but instead adapt to different contexts by developing specialized modules of meanings and competencies that might or might not be integrated into more comprehensive systems (Kelly, 1955/1991). Each of these points finds expression in postmodern understandings of psychological disorder, the topic to which we shall now turn.

9

# Contextualizing disorder

In general, postmodern psychotherapists tend to shy away from traditional diagnosis, although they recognize its necessity to satisfy the demands of insurance companies and managed health care organizations. This cautiousness about formal diagnosis is in reaction to an objectivistic, reductionistic, modernist way of defining people by their disorder rather than by their unique ways of approaching life difficulties. Although linguistically it may be convenient to refer to a client with profound difficulties with interpersonal relationships, fear of real or imagined abandonment, and self-harm tendencies as a "borderline," doing so does little to expand the choices available to this client or to the therapist who works with her or him (Harter, 1995). Thus, postmodern psychotherapists will allow formal diagnosis to inform their therapeutic practice, but not limit its scope.

This ambivalence about traditional diagnosis notwithstanding, postmodern psychotherapists make use of a number of distinctive problem formulations at different levels of the epigenetic hierarchy from the biogenetic to the cultural. However, they do so with the awareness that these diagnoses themselves are human constructions (Raskin & Lewandowski, 2000) that are helpful to some clients and not others, and to some therapists and not others. For instance, Joanne's diagnosis of "panic attacks of psychogenic origin" in the opening case example was not useful in helping her to understand her paralyzing anxiety, although for a different client such a diagnosis might provide sufficient rationale for the anxious feelings experienced, and offer a frame of reference for working on the resultant symptomatology. Regardless, it is the interplay between the client and the therapist that guides the utility of formal diagnoses for a particular client, as well as the interplay between the different levels of the hierarchy that informs the diagnostic process. The tendency of postmodern psychotherapy to consider how these levels interact distinguishes it from psychiatric and psychotherapeutic approaches that focus on only the lower end of the continuum—the bio-genetic and the personal-agentic levels—as more traditional cognitive therapies tend to do. Understanding that a combination of factors may be contributing to personal difficulties allows the psychotherapist multiple avenues for problem exploration. Thus, in this Point I will describe a general approach to understanding "disorder" at all four levels, deferring discussions of specific problem conceptualizations associated with various constructivist, social constructionist, and narrative perspectives until later in the book, when they can be anchored in more detailed case examples.

At the *bio-genetic level*, constructivist psychotherapists recognize that some personal difficulties can have physiological origins. As is true with all "best practices" of psychotherapy, it is important for practitioners to identify physiological causes of distress (thyroid difficulties in mood disorder, blood flow difficulties in erectile dysfunction, etc.). For this reason, referrals for medical evaluation are not in principle problematic, although a pharmacological approach to treatment is rarely regarded as sufficient in itself. In Joanne's case, a medical evaluation had already been obtained, and it was the lack of a biogenetic causal factor for her symptoms that prompted her to present for therapy when she did. In fact, in this situation, it was not necessary to focus much therapeutic attention on her physical complaints, as the meaning of her symptoms was discovered in the personal-agentic and dyadic-relational realms.

On the *personal-agentic level*, diagnostic attention is paid to personal ways of making meaning that have not been revised to meet the changing needs of lived experiences. Indeed, the founding figure of clinical constructivism, George Kelly (1955/

1991), described disorder as any construction that continues to be used despite repeatedly having proven itself a failure. Often personal constructions of "how things work" in the world were created during the individual's early years of meaning making, and, although they may have been useful guides at that time, they may have lost their utility in current life situations. For example, a child may learn early on that having someone get angry with her/him means a loss of love or attention, so she/he works to be "good" and not misbehave. Yet, as an adult, avoiding all anger from anyone may result in non-assertive behavior, feelings of low self-worth, and relational difficulties. Thus, a revision of the initial construction of "anger means loss" may lead to a more adaptive way of making life meaning. Note that the revision of life meanings is a co-constructed process between the client and the therapist, and the choice of revision (and the direction it takes) is the sole propriety of the client. For Joanne, the feelings of guilt and disloyalty she experienced by wanting to pursue her own dreams and by moving away from her home community resulted from core constructs concerning her roles in her family of origin, her current family, and the African-American church community to which she belonged. Allowing herself a wider range of options for construing her roles with those closest to her lessened both her feelings of guilt and the resultant panic-like symptomatology.

Like the personal-agentic level, the *dyadic-relational level* is concerned with meaning-making processes. However, at this level diagnostic attention is paid to the interaction between clients and those most relevant to them in their current life or in the past. In particular, the ability (or inability) of the client to enter into genuine role relationships (Leitner, Faidley, & Celantana, 2000) entailing the cultivation of deep and meaningful intimacies with another person is explored. Additionally, the ways in which each partner either validates or invalidates the meaning-making processes of the other can lead to diagnostically rich information when searching for problematic patterns in couples relationships, as depicted in the assessment section below. Importantly, relational difficulties do not have to be with people currently in the client's life. As was especially significant in Joanne's case, postmodern therapists consider the possibility that a problematic relationship can still exist with someone who is no longer living, in a way that hampers current adjustment. For Joanne, the externally imposed removal of her father from her life contributed to her difficulty in adapting to her new city, and reconnection with him following the chair work freed her to have a more "real" life with those around her. Although some other forms of cognitive therapy reach toward the world of relationship, constructivism is distinguished by its strong emphasis on the relational co-construction of meaning in its most elemental concepts. In a very important sense, constructivists hold that it is not so much people who construct relationships, but rather relationships that construct people—for better or worse.

At the *cultural-linguistic level*, postmodern therapists pay particular attention to the cultural embeddedness of difficulties in a client's life. Like all embracing meaning systems, the vast and implicit system of signs, symbols, rules, and roles that constitutes culture is a two-edged sword, on the one hand providing a supportive framework within which people can construct a viable sense of identity, but on the other hand limiting the repertoire of possibilities that they can endorse, or even perceive. In Joanne's situation, the guilt she experienced for having desires (for advanced education) that did not fit with the "dominant narrative" of her community (White & Epston, 1990) became a focus of concern as she sought ways of drawing upon her faith tradition while also finding her unique "voice." This implies that postmodern therapists often function as agents of social change, helping clients reinterpret or resist those features of their cultural frameworks that are oppressive for themselves and others (e.g., the "permission" that Western culture gives for men to assert power in intimate relationships). At the same time, postmodern therapists seek not to impose their own preferred culture on the persons with whom they work, instead focusing on and "deconstructing" the inherent contradictions and possibilities that reside within any given cultural framework.

It is important to emphasize the optimism about human potential that underpins many expressions of postmodern therapy. Although the complexity of life—not to mention the complexity of the self—persistently challenges our adaptation, people are ultimately regarded as incipient scientists devising ever more comprehensive and adequate theories of life (Kelly, 1955/1991), as authoritative authors of their own life stories (White & Epston, 1990), and as deliberate discourse users (Harré & Gillett, 1994) who selectively draw upon the store-house of available cultural forms to craft satisfying ways of "moving forward" at individual and social levels. This respectful stance toward clients finds expression in all aspects of therapy, from spontaneous forms of assessment in sessions to carefully planned experiments with alternative identities in daily life, as I will illustrate below.

Because of the very broad set of approaches and methods that fall under the postmodern constructivist umbrella, it is difficult to identify a population to which such approaches have *not* been applied. Nonetheless, postmodern therapists are typically less enthusiastic than their cognitive-behavioral colleagues about defining diagnostic categories of clients to whom their approaches are particularly relevant. In part, this reluctance expresses their ethical commitment to the uniqueness of the client and the recognition that generic categories of people provide little useful guidance in how to intervene with a given person confronting specific difficulties. It is for this reason that constructivist assessment techniques and therapeutic interactions consistently seek to identify that distinctive set of resources and restrictions embodied in the client's activity, so that the therapist and client can draw on the former to address the latter. Sometimes, clients' construction of their selves and situations might suggest the relevance of therapeutic techniques that are less favored by postmodern therapists, such as psycho-educational interactions, which cast therapists in an authoritative teaching role, or behavior therapy, which might encourage the monitoring and modification of very molecular behaviors. Although constructivist therapists can be both flexible and forceful in their intervention style (Efran & Fauber, 1995), and even though studies have shown that constructivists make use of a wider range of psychotherapeutic techniques than more rationalist cognitive therapists (G. J. Neimeyer, Lee, Aksoy-Toska, & Phillip, 2008), in fact, evidence indicates that most prefer a more reflective, participatory style of therapy (Mahoney, 1993; Vasco, 1994) as their primary *modus operandi*. Correspondingly, research on treatment acceptability suggests that potential clients who have an internal locus of control tend to prefer constructivist therapies, whereas those with a more external orientation are more attracted to traditional cognitive or behavioral therapies (Vincent & LeBow, 1995). Likewise, those clients who are inner-directed, open to experience, and define their problems in interpersonal terms tend both to be drawn to and to respond favorably to reflective interventions like those emphasized in this book, whereas those persons who are outer-directed, closed to experience, and conservative—and who correspondingly view their problems as discrete symptoms to be eliminated—have been found to display an affinity for behavior therapy approaches (Winter, 1990). It therefore seems entirely appropriate for an ethical constructivist therapist to appraise the client's dominant modes of experiencing both the self and symptom, and in those instances where these personal factors suggest a mismatch with the therapist's style of work, to recommend referral to another mode of therapy.

# Part 2

# THE DISTINCTIVE PRACTICAL FEATURES OF CPT

In keeping with the epigenetic model, constructivist assessment ranges across the entire spectrum of the person–environment system, with a concentration on those mid-level systems (i.e., the personal-agentic and dyadic-relational) that are of most practical relevance to psychotherapy. However, the focus of clinical work is also informed by assessments conducted at concretely biological and abstractly cultural levels, as it is sometimes critical to understand specific organic etiology (e.g., in cases of neurological impairment, physical illness, or disposition to mood disorder) and broad social factors (e.g., economic disadvantage or racial or gender-based oppression) in order to work effectively with individuals and groups struggling with intransient problems. But even in these cases, constructivist and social constructionist approaches are characterized by attention to the personal and social meanings that characterize and constrain clients presenting for help, as illustrated by

Sacks' (1998) evocative exploration of the phenomenological worlds of patients with brain injury or Brown's (2000a) insightful critique of broad social and linguistic factors that limit the identity options available to women.

In the clinical context, this inclination toward multi-systemic assessment means that postmodern therapists sometimes use conventional diagnostic categories (e.g., bipolar disorder, schizophrenia), particularly when these help sensitize the clinician to bio-genetic features of the problem that might require attention. But this is typically done only cautiously and conditionally, with the recognition that psychiatric diagnoses are themselves fallible human constructions that provide only a crude orientation to the client's difficulties (Raskin & Lewandowski, 2000). As a result, much more fine-grained assessment of the client's world of meaning is required to reveal his or her individuality, distinctive difficulties, and relevant resources. My goal in this part is to introduce several such procedures, pointing the reader toward additional sources (Fransella, Bell, & Bannister, 2004; G. J. Neimeyer, 1993) for a fuller presentation of related methods.

As is true for proponents of many other process-oriented approaches to psychotherapy, postmodern therapists prefer to blur the distinction between evaluation and intervention, arguing that the most useful forms of assessment enhance the awareness of both client and therapist regarding relevant themes, issues, difficulties, and resources (R. A. Neimeyer, 1993c). As such, they rarely take the form of "stand alone" procedures completed prior to therapy, but instead tend to be introduced in the course of therapy at points when they have the potential to be not only clarifying but also change generating. Here I will present and illustrate a few of the methods used by constructivist, narrative, and social constructionist therapists, some of which will also play a role in the detailed case study presented later in the book.

10

# Laddering toward core concerns

First introduced by Hinkle (1965), laddering represents an assessment strategy at the personal-agentic level that directly elicits hierarchical features of the individual's personal construct system, linking concrete perceptions, behaviors or role descriptions with the higher-order issues they imply. As such, it is frequently helpful in the course of therapy for deepening a client's inquiry into a particular complaint or revealing subtle ways in which a person's sense of self becomes tied up with a symptom. Conversely, as is true for most constructivist methods, it can also help identify important client values and strengths that can provide anchoring points for a "preferred self" (Eron & Lund, 1996), in keeping with the precept that every meaning system embodies both problems and prospects, and the most effective therapy entails drawing on the latter to address the former.

Laddering can begin with nearly any personal construct (Kelly, 1955/1991), or significant personal contrast, that is of interest in the course of therapy. For example, in discussing an ongoing conflict between her parents, a client might describe her father as the *ambitious* one. Sensitized to the implicit contrast, the therapist might then prompt, ". . . whereas your mother is more . . . ," to which the client might reply, "Well, she's more *content with herself*." This construct, *ambitious vs. content with self*, might then become the first "rung" in a ladder that could be "climbed" further through the pattern of questioning described and illustrated below. Alternatively, a client could describe paralyzing indecision about whether to *stay in a familiar job* (or relationship) or *pursue something different*. Again, this contrast could be explored through the laddering procedure, tracing the implications of each alternative. Finally, laddering can be useful in exploring conflicting aspects of oneself, such as antagonistic feelings, actions, or features of one's personality. Something of the sort was done in the clinical vignette that follows.

Essentially, laddering consists of a series of straightforward, recursive questions, in which the therapist first identifies an initial bi-polar construct, and then asks with which of the poles the client prefers to associate him- or herself. The therapist writes down the construct, notes the client's preference, and then asks either, "Why?" or, "What is the advantage of that?" (or a linguistic variation) to elicit the higher-order implication of this choice. Connecting the preferred pole to its implied higher-order construct with an arrow, the therapist then requests the opposite or contrast, and aligns it with the previous non-preferred pole. The therapist continues in this way, inquiring about a preference, a reason or advantage, and its contrast in a cyclical pattern of questioning until the client begins repeating responses or finds it difficult to formulate a further construct. The depiction of the final ladder then can be shared with the client to further mutual inquiry into this hierarchy of meanings and what they imply for his or her behavior. The ladder resulting from the interview segment that follows is depicted in Figure 2. Use of techniques like laddering to depict how a client's thoughts fit together in hierarchies of meaning converging on core issues is unique to constructivist therapy, highlighting the point that the connections between people's constructs are as important as the constructs themselves.

Michael D was a married, 45-year-old salesman who sought therapy for a nagging depression, which he related to the "emptiness" of his life. Although remarkably buoyant and jocular with office staff, he soon responded to my sympathetic seriousness as a therapist by hesitantly acknowledging his loneliness and avoidance of close relationships. When asked for his "personal theory" about the persistence of this problem in his life, Michael responded by saying that he thought it was

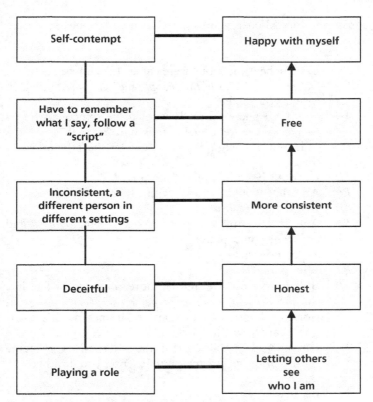

**Figure 2** Personal construct ladder for Michael D

related to his tendency to "play a role" with everyone he knew, even in supposedly intimate relationships, like his marriage. Seeking clarification of this important construct through contrast, I asked, "And what would be the opposite of that stance, playing a role?" Michael quickly glanced away, and after a few seconds of silence, again met my eyes and said, "Just letting people see who I am." Tears immediately followed.

Struck by the emotional poignancy of this experiential contrast, I decided to tease out the deeper implications of this construct for Michael through the use of the laddering interview.

> *Bob (B):* Michael, if you were able to choose between *playing a role* and *letting people see who you are*, which would you prefer?
>
> *Michael (M):* I guess I'd really want to be someone who *let people see me for who I am*, as hard as that is.
>
> *B:* Can you say why? What would be the advantage of that?
>
> *M:* It would be more *honest*, more *real*.
>
> *B:* And that would contrast with . . . ?
>
> *M:* Just being *deceitful*.
>
> *B:* And faced with a choice between being *honest* and *deceitful*, you'd prefer . . . .
>
> *M:* To be honest.
>
> *B:* Why is that?
>
> *M:* Because it would let me be more *consistent*. I feel like I'm *inconsistent, a different person in every setting*—at work, at home, and in social relationships. It's like I don't carry the same person from place to place.
>
> *B:* Hmm. And so faced with the alternatives of being *consistent* or *inconsistent* in that sense, you'd rather . . .?
>
> *M:* Be consistent.
>
> *B:* Because . . . .
> *(Thoughtful pause)*
>
> *M:* Because then I would feel *free*, instead of feeling like I have to remember what I said in each relationship, like I have to remember my *script*.
>
> *B:* And choosing between that *scripted* kind of interaction, and that sort of *freedom* . . . ?
>
> *M:* I'd want to be *free*.
>
> *B:* Can you say why?
>
> *M:* Hmm . . . .
> *(Long pause)*
>
> *M:* Because then I could be . . . *happy with myself*.

*B:*    And the contrast to that is . . . ?

*M:*    Just . . . *self-contempt*. The truth is, I have contempt for people who are like I am. Someday I'd like to be able just to laugh genuinely and not have to work at it, force it for, um, social effect.

Concluding the ladder, Michael then confessed, tears rolling down his cheeks, "You're the first person in 45 years I've ever told, ever acknowledged that my life is a lie."

Once completed, the ladder can flow smoothly into discussion of its deeper themes (in Michael's case, touching on his self-contempt about his ultimate deceitfulness, and his yearning for a sense of freedom from the artificiality of his contrived self-presentations to others). Alternatively, the therapist can sharpen the focus on the client's sense of self-congruence or self-contradiction by going back and asking the client where he or she *actually* would place him- or herself on each of the constructs, revealing points of compatibility or conflict between actual and preferred self-views. Finally, the therapist could draw selectively on any of a number of "facilitative questions" for prompting further processing of the ladder with the client, either in session or in the form of written "homework" between appointments (see Table 1). Significantly, some of these questions nudge this personal-agentic assessment technique in the direction of a dyadic-relational exploration. Further instructions in the clinical use of laddering, along with discussion of more complex patterns of conflict or ambivalence, are provided by R. A. Neimeyer (1993c) and R. A. Neimeyer, Anderson, and Stockton (2001). The latter authors also provide empirical evidence that laddering does indeed shift the client to more abstract, existentially rich themes that may be hard to formulate in words, just as constructivist theory would predict.

**Table 1** Facilitative questions for exploring personal construct ladders

---

- What central values are implied by the ideas you align yourself with at the upper end of your ladder? How would these be expressed in specific behaviors, traits, or roles at the lower end of the ladder? Who in your life best exemplifies your "preferred self" view?
- Were there points at which you hesitated before assigning a pole preference? What might have been going on for you at that point?
- Who in your life most supports/most resists the preferences you describe?
- Which of these preferences are visible/invisible to others? To whom? What might this say about your important relationships?
- Have there ever been times in your life when you would have placed yourself or your values at the opposite poles of these constructs? What was your life like at that time?
- What could be some positive connotations for your non-preferred poles? Are there any cases in which you could see a value in integrating these opposites in some fashion? What might such a life look like?

---

*Source*: Adapted from Neimeyer, R. A., Anderson, A. and Stockton, L. (2001) "Snakes versus ladders: A validation of laddering technique as a measure of hierarchical structure", *Journal of Constructivist Psychology*, 14: 85–105.

# Mapping social ecologies of meaning using the bow-tie interview

First developed by Procter (1987), the bow-tie interview is situated at the juncture of the personal-agentic and dyadic-relational levels of the epigenetic model, linking personal processes of meaning making to the delicate social ecology of intimate interpersonal relationships that sustain them. It is particularly useful as a means of clarifying complex interactive sequences in conflicted couples and families, and in suggesting a roadmap for intervention. As such, it might be viewed as a variety of *circular questioning*—therapeutic questions that reveal relationships between members of a family—as pioneered by family therapists sharing a concern with the social construction of meaning (Hoffman, 1992). Like the strategies of these postmodern family therapists, bow-tie work entails elaborating the *position* of each member of the problematic system or subsystem, defined as the integrated stance that each person takes at the levels of construction and action. That is, at any given moment of interaction, family members both construe one another in certain ways, and behave in a way that is coherent with that construction. At the same time, the behaviors or actions of each serve to validate or invalidate the other's construction of their relationship, in a seamless cycle of meaning and action that has no clear beginning or end. This emphasis on how an individual's construction of meaning and action dovetails with that of relevant others highlights the strongly *social* and *relational* character of constructivist therapy, in contrast to the more individualistic emphases of other cognitive approaches.

An illustration of this method of assessment is provided with Ken and Donna, a couple in their twenties who sought treatment from a university counseling center for explosive arguments that were threatening their two-year-old marriage. As the trainee therapist I was supervising felt quite "stuck" in knowing how to deal with their apparent standoff, I immediately thought of the bow-tie interview as a way to introduce clarity into their sessions, offer some perspective and insight to the conflicted couple, and assist the beleaguered therapist in thinking of interventions that could begin to cut through the knots that bound the couple in escalating cycles of confrontation and retreat. Stumped in her own efforts, the therapist eagerly accepted any coaching I was able to provide.

Rather than a standard series of questions like those that constitute the laddering interview, bow-tie interviews are structured more fluidly, beginning with any of the four foci that together comprise the bow tie of the problem (i.e., the constructions or actions that characterize either of the partners). In this case, the obvious starting point was provided by the complaint with which Donna opened their first therapy session, a session she had pushed her accountant husband to attend despite his initial reluctance. Clearly frustrated with Ken's sullen silence, Donna detailed her concerns, which focused on his "shutting her out" and "pushing her away." As a psychology major at the university, she said, she knew that healthy relationships needed to include the sharing of feelings, but she felt increasingly that she had to "dig to reach him on an emotional level." As the therapist explored what Donna was seeking in the relationship, she emphasized her need for "real companionship," something that she more consistently found with friends in the university drama club than with her husband. In response to the therapist's inquiry about how she found herself acting on the basis of these perceptions of the relationship, Donna acknowledged that she would often "press Ken to discuss their problems," and, as he stonewalled her efforts, she would spend more time with university friends to meet her social needs.

Turning to Ken, the therapist then inquired how he made sense of his wife's behavior. Ken's frustration was palpable as he replied, "All she does is complain about our marriage. It's clear that she cares more about her friends than she does about me." Gently prompted to put into words his concerns about the relationship, Ken further disclosed his fear that his wife was, ". . . probably having an affair and planning to desert him." In response to the therapist's query about how he found himself acting on the basis of this interpretation of the relationship, Ken conceded that he would withdraw angrily and then periodically explode when Donna would spend evenings away from home. Both partners acknowledged that this cycle had amplified in recent months, though each characteristically blamed the other for its occurrence.

The bow tie of Donna and Ken's positions is diagrammed in Figure 3. Although the natural structure of the session led the therapist to start with Donna's construction of the relationship, in fact the cycle had no clear point of origin that would lead to the attribution of blame to either partner. Instead, each had done his or her part in maintaining the predictable "dance" of their interaction, as the actions of each validated the constructions of the other, which led coherently to that individual's further actions, which further validated the partner's anticipations and interpretations, and so on, without interruption. Looking at the diagram offered by the therapist, with the recurring cycle traced repeatedly by her finger following the looping arrows of their exchange, both partners felt understood, and sensed that an apparently chaotic marriage actually had a clear, if painful, predictability. Each also began to grasp, at least in a preliminary way, the meanings of the partner's actions in his or her own terms, and each was more ready to consider thinking about ways to "break the cycle." Indeed, the bow-tie diagram provided a kind of template for further intervention, insofar as altering any aspect of the cycle—whether at the level of behavior change in either partner, reframing the meaning of their interaction, empathically entering the partner's interpretation of their respective actions, or developing more complex "hybrid" interventions across levels or partners—would interrupt the

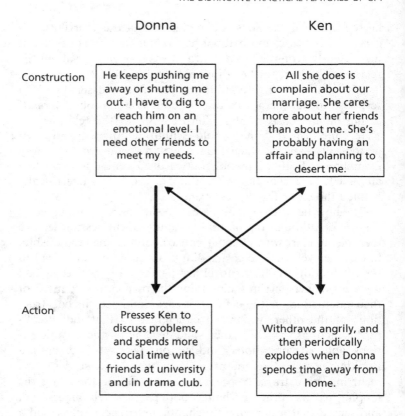

**Figure 3** "Bow tie" linking levels of construction and action for a distressed couple

pernicious pattern and offer "news of a difference" in the relationship (Bateson, 1972). More detailed case studies involving multiple members of a family system are provided by Feixas (1995) and R. A. Neimeyer (1993c).

12

# Charting networks of constructs using repertory grids

First proposed by Kelly (1955/1991) and extended by subsequent generations of personal construct theorists, *repertory grid technique* represents a flexible method for eliciting those personal dimensions of meaning that a client uses to structure some important domain of experience. By requesting that the respondent compare and contrast a relevant set of "elements" (e.g., family members, alternative careers, or parts of the body), grid technique prompts the person to give voice to the personal constructs that he or she uses to organize that aspect of life. Although the resulting constructs can be revealing at a clinical or impressionistic level (e.g., finding that a preponderance of one's constructs are concerned with themes of *external compulsion* versus *personal resistance*, or with being *one up* versus *one down*), reliable formal systems of content coding have been devised to analyze construct content into categories (e.g., moral, emotional, relational, concrete) for both clinical and research purposes (Feixas, Geldschlager, & Neimeyer, 2002). Furthermore, by rating each element on the respondent's own construct dimensions and analyzing the resulting ratings using any of a number of automated programs (Fransella et al., 2004), the clinician can obtain a quick and comprehensive visual mapping of meaning that the client uses to structure her or his experience of a relevant domain, such as the interpersonal world. Thus, rather than having the client respond to standardized questions constructed by the psychologist, grid technique in essence invites clients to construct their own questionnaire through first determining the constructs, and then using them to rate or rank the relevant elements. This capacity to yield a highly personal but systematic glimpse of the client's construction of the world, in combination with the ease of administration of computerized grid analysis programs available at no cost through the Internet,[1] help account for the technique's widespread usage in both clinical and non-clinical applications, ranging from cognitive psychology (Adams-Webber, 2001) to vocational development (G. J. Neimeyer, 1992). For our purposes, it is also worth noting that grid techniques have been used to assess aspects of all four levels of the epigenetic model, spanning bodily experiences such as the body-constructs of cancer patients (Weber, Bronner, Their, Kingreen, & Klapp, 2000), self-roles of depressed clients (R. A. Neimeyer, Klein, Gurman, & Greist, 1983), family relationships (Feixas, 1992), and broad cultural attitudes (G. J. Neimeyer & Fukuyama, 1984). Variations on the method, such as *implications grids* and *resistance-to-change grids* (Dempsey & Neimeyer, 1995; Hinkle, 1965) provide additional means of identifying core constructs that define the client's key value commitments, which, paradoxically, often constrain their change in psychotherapy. This attempt to assess complex systems of meaning using rigorous cognitive assessment methods sets personal construct theory apart from other approaches to cognitive therapy that focus simply on self-statements or schemas derived from simple self-report. An easy guide to the construction and use of repertory grids in applied settings is provided by Jankowicz (2003).

1 See, for example, the popular WebGrid III program available at http:// tiger.cpsc.ucalgary.ca/.

13

## Assessing emotional and relational themes using self-confrontation

A somewhat related technique is the *self-confrontation method* or SCM (Hermans, 2002), an approach to personality investigation in which clients are asked to formulate "valuations," or positive/ negative assessments of important events and circumstances in their lives, and then rate them on a set of provided scales that measure a range of emotional responses to these events, as well as the degree of *personal agency* or *communion* with other people implied by them. This assessment begins with certain prompting questions to elicit a set of 6 or 8 valuations, such as: "Was there something in your past that has been of major importance for your life and that still plays an important part today?" or, "Is there a goal or objective that you expect to play an important role in your future life?" In response to the first question, for example, a client might say, "I've always tried to 'be there' for friends and family, even when this has hurt me in terms of my commitment to my work or career." Ratings on the provided scales might then suggest that this valuation is associated with strong positive emotions such as *love* and *joy* and high levels of communion or connection with others. In contrast, the same client might assign quite different meanings to the competing valuation, "I am having to limit my involvement with my wife and children in order to attend to the consistent demands of my boss and clients," rating it as involving strong negative affect (e.g., *despondency* and *disappointment*) and low communion (e.g., low *intimacy* and *tenderness*). A somewhat simplified adaptation of this method appears in Table 2.

**Table 2** Instructions for the self-confrontation method

The Dutch psychologist Hubert Hermans devised the self-confrontation method (SCM) as a humanistic means of teasing out and reflecting upon the basic themes and motives implied in one's self-narrative or personal story. It entails first identifying key subjective construals of life experiences, which he called *valuations*, and then rating these on a series of affective terms. The matrix of ratings can then be analyzed further to prompt further reflections on the general significance of these emotionally significant experiences.

Start this abbreviated form of the SCM by formulating brief responses to the following questions, striving to capture the essence of the valuation in one or two sentences:

*Past*

1   What is something of major significance in my past that continues to exert a strong influence on me?
2   Was there any person or circumstance that greatly influenced my life and still appreciably affects my life now?

*Present*

3   What in my present life is of major importance, and exerts a significant influence on me?
4   Is there any present person or circumstance that plays a significant role in my life?

*Future*

5   Do I foresee anything or anyone in my future that will exert a major influence on my life?
6   Is there any major goal that I expect to play an important role in my life in the future? You can look as far ahead as you wish.

For example, someone might respond to the first question, "My parents' divorce, which left me feeling that all close relationships can end unpredictably," or to the third with, "I resist the attempts of my major professor to control and determine what I should be doing." Obviously, the only "right answers" to these questions are the ones that speak honestly from within your experience.

Now rate each of your valuations on the following affect scales, assigning a number of 0 to 5 to each on a scale ranging from 0 = *not at all* to 5 = *very much*. For example, for the second valuation above regarding resisting control, someone might rate it a 4 on "pride," 0 on "intimacy," 1 on "inner calm," and 3 on "disappointment." It is probably useful to take a moment to sit quietly for a minute and simply "feel" your way into a valuation, and then work down the column for it, rating it on each term. You can then take a moment to clear your mind, conjure up the affective tone of the next valuation, and move on to the next column. Conclude by rating your "general feelings" now, at this point in your life, and your "ideal feelings."

| Valuation: | | 1 | 2 | 3 | 4 | 5 | 6 | General | Ideal |
|---|---|---|---|---|---|---|---|---|---|
| Strength (S) | | | | | | | | | |
| Love (O) | | | | | | | | | |
| Joy (P) | | | | | | | | | |
| Worry (N) | | | | | | | | | |
| Self-confidence (S) | | | | | | | | | |
| Tenderness (O) | | | | | | | | | |
| Enjoyment (P) | | | | | | | | | |
| Unhappiness (N) | | | | | | | | | |
| Pride (S) | | | | | | | | | |
| Intimacy (O) | | | | | | | | | |
| Inner calm (P) | | | | | | | | | |
| Disappointment (N) | | | | | | | | | |
| | S total: | | | | | | | | |
| | O total: | | | | | | | | |
| | P total: | | | | | | | | |
| | N total: | | | | | | | | |

When you have finished, add up the ratings for each column for the S (self-enhancement), O (contact with others), P (positive), and N (negative) indices, including the "general feelings" and "ideal feelings" columns. Add up your ratings for all 6 basic valuations (excluding general and ideal), compute the mean (simply dividing by 6), and compare your profile with the following configurations, defining "high" as a rating of 8 or above, and "low" as ratings of 7 or below. Then compare your profile with the following categories:

- *High S, O & P; low N:* Hermans identifies this as a profile of "unity and strength," being high in self-enhancement and communion with others.
- *High O & P; low S & N:* This connotes "unity and love," finding meaning in union with others, but with diminished self-efficacy.
- *High O & N; low S & P:* The profile reflects "unfulfilled longing," a

yearning for communion with others coupled with low personal confidence.

- *High N; low S, O & P:* This is the configuration of "powerlessness and isolation," marked by personal as well as interpersonal desolation.
- *High S & N; low O & P:* Hermans describes this as a profile of "aggression and anger," in which self-assertion occurs in the face of a disappointing world.
- *High S & P; low O & N:* This describes a pattern of "autonomy and success," against a backdrop of low connection with others.

Note that the more extreme your scores are, the better your valuations might be described in these terms, with small differences between high and low values suggesting caution in interpretation of the profile. Note also that some possible configurations will fall outside the typology or represent "mixed types."

Now that you have assessed your profile, reflect on the following questions:

- What in my life has contributed to my development of these affective themes? Do I imagine this changing in the future, and if so, how?
- Looking at individual valuations, do they appear basically unchanging across all six questions or rather variable in their individual profiles? Are there any sharp differences among the configurations for past, present and future valuations? If so, what might this signify?
- How well does my profile correspond to my sense of the deep themes of my life, in terms of my feelings about myself and social world? If there is a mismatch, how might I explain it?
- If I compared the above profile for the 6 valuations with an SOPN profile calculated for the single "general feelings" column, how closely would they match? Again, if there is a significant discrepancy, what might this mean?
- How do each of these two profiles (the mean column and the general) compare to that for the "ideal feelings" column? If there is a discrepancy, what does this say about how I might like my life narrative to change? How might I strive to reduce the gap between my current and ideal valuations in this case?
- What advantages and disadvantages might I see to using the self-confrontation in a clinical assessment context?

*Source*: Adapted from Hermans, H. (2002) "The person as a motivated storyteller," in R. A. Neimeyer and G. J. Neimeyer (eds), *Advances in Personal Construct Psychology*, Vol. 5. Westport, CN: Praeger.

Completion of the self-confrontation method at various points across the course of counseling can therefore help crystallize issues demanding therapeutic attention, while also inviting the client to function as a co-investigator in the therapeutic relationship, as illustrated by Hermans (1995). In this way the SCM functions as a clinical assessment technique situated principally at the personal-agentic level of the epigenetic model. Like other approaches to narrative therapy described below, the self-confrontation method also tends to take a longitudinal view of the client's life story by teasing out major aspects of its unfolding plot and theme. In this way it complements traditional cognitive approaches to assessment, which tend to focus more narrowly on what clients are "telling themselves now," in the midst of stressful situations.

14

# Reflecting on the self using mirror time

Specific assessment procedures can be especially appropriate when assigned as homework, often blending an attempt to tap into and make more visible or audible a client's processes of meaning making with a therapeutic intent to promote change-inducing self-dialogue. An illustration of such arose in the context of work with a young woman named Kristin undergoing a period of exploration of self and career who expressed intrigue at my suggestion of using Mahoney's (1991) mirror time as a means of quite literally reflecting upon herself at an important life juncture. The procedure involves spending a specified period of time before a mirror in a private setting, perhaps accompanied by reflective instrumental music. Depending on the technique's intended focus, the client can be encouraged to allow her or his attention to range freely, or be given a set of guiding instructions (e.g., to allow parts of the self to pose relevant questions and other parts to provide answers, or to shift awareness to different parts of the face or body). Likewise, the feelings and reflections that arise during and after the exercise can be recorded in a free-form journal entry immediately afterward, or simply noted for later therapeutic discussion. An adaptation of mirror time instructions appears in Table 3.

In the present case, Kristin accepted my invitation to spend 30 minutes in front of a mirror guided by taped instructions. In response to these instructions, Kristin penned a poignant set of reflections, portions of which follow:

Birthmark below my left eye; no, my right eye. Strange how I am seeing myself opposite from how the world sees me.

**Table 3** Instructions for mirror time exercise

Seek a private place and time, where you can be undisturbed for at least 30 minutes. Then sit in front of a mirror, perhaps on a barstool, in a way that you can see yourself comfortably from your shoulders up, or better, in a full-length mirror. Then simply follow the instructions below, which you might wish to tape record in your own voice and play back as you make use of the mirror, pausing for a couple of minutes between questions (represented by ellipses in written text) to allow reflection:

> Gently observe what your attention is first drawn to as you look in the mirror. . . . Witness what you are thinking, imagining, feeling. . . . Look deeply into your own eyes. . . . What do you see? . . . What do you like and dislike as you view this person? . . . Are there any differences between the person in the mirror and the person you sense yourself to be? . . . What do you see in this face, this person, that others do not?

Now open your eyes, and pause the tape recorder if you have chosen to use one. Try to capture the flow of feelings, observations, and answers to the above questions while they remain fresh, noting them briefly on paper. Then return to the further instructions below:

> Close your eyes for several seconds and take a few slow, relaxing breaths. . . . Set your intentions to be self-aware and self-caring. . . . Then slowly open your eyes, inviting yourself to open to the possibility of seeing yourself in a different way. . . . Speaking aloud, quietly ask yourself the question, "Who are you?" . . . Allow this dialogue to continue in whatever way it does, letting the questioning part of you wait patiently for an answer, as another part formulates a response. . . . What do you most need to ask yourself in this moment of honesty, and what do you most need to hear?

After spending several minutes in such reflections, again note them on paper. Finish by summarizing these in a piece of reflective writing that touches on these themes, beginning with what your attention was drawn toward, and then progressing to the sorts of feelings, thoughts, and possible recognitions or insights stimulated by the exercise.

*Source*: Adapted from M. J. Mahoney (1991) *Human Change Processes*. New York: Basic Books.

The freckle on my nose that everyone mistakes for a nose ring. Lots of freckles. Dark circles. Lopsided eyebrows. Wrinkles on my forehead, a new addition. Huge pupils.

I blink and feel the dryness of my contact lenses. I move my jaw to feel its repetitive popping, reminding me of the doctor's words, "mandible worn straight on one side," "permanent damage," and the X-ray on which my cartilage, instead of looking like a thin rainbow stretching in between this delicate joint, looked like a little misplaced bean. I rub my eye out of habit and press my chapped lips. I try to imagine perfect vision and a perfect temporal mandibular joint. But I find it easier to experience the dull throb and dry eyes. To feel the familiar.

I am in fifth grade. I am 25. I see the fifth grader. I see the young adult. I am beautiful. I am plain. I see both. This is how the world sees me. This is how no one sees me. Not smiling. Not laughing or talking. I open my eyes wide and let air pass under my contact lenses, then blink and my image blurs.

I like who I see because she knows me. I feel right in her skin. I dislike her because she doesn't have the answers I want. She stares back at me with too many emotions and not enough wisdom. I like her because she's not falling apart and because she sometimes makes people happy. I don't like her because she's unsure.

I see fear behind her look of resolve. This person is scared and still. Quiet and sad. I'm none of those things.

I let myself exist with a number of different possibilities for who I am. Worker, child, daughter, sister, friend, room-mate, lover—none of them is how I define myself. I participate in life experiences like . . . a traveler. I am a traveler.

Which makes it strange, then, that when I asked myself, "What do you want from life?" the answer was, "Purpose." This apparent contradiction between who I am and what I want from life was resolved through realizing that I have been traveling through my life experiences in search of my purpose. Even as a child the question, "What am I here to do?" has been the one driving me. And so I traveled, literally and figuratively, through life. I found my answer working with emotionally troubled girls. I finally felt right in life. I knew why I was here when I worked with those girls . . . . Because I don't want to travel forever.

I ended my time making funny faces in the mirror. This is a favorite pastime of mine, and good therapy for anyone in need of a laugh.

As Kristin's journal illustrates, this deceptively simple method, if offered and accepted in the right spirit, can facilitate deep-going self-reflection that can be productive in itself, or easily be integrated into an ongoing therapeutic conversation. Like many constructivist methods, it equally embodies the goals of self-assessment and therapeutic assessment, making more vivid and evident how a client might experience herself when her attention is directed inward and away from the social world. What emerges is a distinctive orientation to assessment that has more in common with psychodynamic free association than the highly constrained responses to questionnaires devised by psychologists that typify other approaches to cognitive therapy. Systematic research on nearly 100 users of this technique confirms that mirror time can be "strong medicine," producing significant increases in both physiological arousal as assessed by galvanic skin response and in subjective tension during the period of actual mirror use (Williams, Diehl, & Mahoney, 2002). It is noteworthy that "scripting" the mirror time with instructions—rather than leaving the encounter with self unguided—dampened women's self-criticism and also produced more favorable responses to the exercise as a therapeutic assignment.

The selection of assessment procedures I have described represents only a small sampling of the innovative qualitative and quantitative means of exploring a client's processes and structures of meaning making devised or adapted by creative constructivists (e.g., Leitner, 1995; G. J. Neimeyer, 1993; R. A. Neimeyer & Winter, 2006). As a group, they tend to be more *holistic* than most approaches to cognitive assessment, in the sense that they shed light on the deeply personal, yet intricately social systems of emotionally resonant meanings, choices, and life narratives that both shape and limit a client's engagement with life. It is to the explicit transformation of these systems that we will now turn.

15

## Attending from self to other

As my colleagues and I have argued elsewhere (Levitt, Neimeyer, & Williams, 2005), clinicians and clients are best served when prescriptions for practice are nested within broader principles that facilitate intelligent judgments about their relevance in a specific setting. This point is less obvious than one might think, in a day characterized by enthusiasm for "rule-governed, reliable and replicable" interventions (Held, 1995), conjuring the image of a therapy bleached of the idiosyncrasy of individual variation, capable of being delivered by essentially interchangeable "providers" of a standardized service. In contrast to cognitive-behavioral therapies advocating such manual-guided approaches to practice with their penchant toward particular protocols, specific agendas, and approved lists of techniques, constructivists emphasize the inherent individuality of therapy and its necessary tailoring to the immediacy of the encounter between *this* therapist working with *this* client at *this* moment of emergent understanding of the problem before them. In such a subjective, shifting, and subtle setting, abstract principles provide better orientation than concrete prescriptions. For this reason I will focus on a trio of principles—the "3 Ps of practice"—that frame my view of therapy, emphasizing those features under each that tend to distinguish the work of constructivist therapists from that of their cognitive-behavioral cousins. I will begin with some remarks about the therapist's *presence* and then move on to a consideration of therapeutic *processes* and clinical *procedures*, illustrating each with vignettes from my own practice.

Therapy begins with who we are, and extends to what we do. That is, bringing *ourselves* to the encounter, as fully as needed, is the essential precondition for all that follows, that distinctive blend of processes and procedures that broadly defines a given therapeutic tradition and more specifically defines our own therapeutic style. Here, I want to emphasize the foundational quality of therapeutic presence, the way in which the offer of full availability to the client's concerns, undistracted by other agendas, grounds the work by offering a reflective audience to the telling and performance of the client's self-narrative, allowing both (or, in the case of family or group therapy, all) participants to take perspective on current conundrums in fresh ways.

In this conception the presence of the therapist does not "crowd out" attention to the client, or even compete with it in a direct sense, as in implying that therapists should be particularly self-disclosing in their work, or offer clients object lessons from their own lives. Instead, it more typically implies a kind of *from–to* attention, as the therapist attends from his or her sense of self to the person of the client. It is precisely this form of "personal knowledge" that is described by the philosopher of science Michael Polanyi (1958), in which the knower holds him- or herself in subsidiary awareness while retaining a focal attention on the other. For example, in a recent session I found myself conducting a (minimally) guided imagery exercise with a client who was grieving the loss of her mother. Inviting her to close her eyes with me, I asked her to scan her body for a felt sense (Gendlin, 1996) of how she was holding the loss, slowing the pace of my instructions to encourage a "loosening" of her meaning making from the more clipped, "tightened" discourse of our previous therapeutic conversation (Kelly, 1955/1991). What emerged was remarkable: with a beatific smile she quickly gestured toward the space around her head, and described a radiant, warm light that seemed to be coming to her from above, beginning to shroud her head and shoulders. Noticing tingles of warmth rippling down my own spine and into my body, I then invited her to allow the light to enter her and envelop her body more completely. As she did so, she brightened still more, nearly laughing, and described a delightful tickling in her abdomen, a sensation strongly reminiscent of how her mother would tickle her when she was a little girl. As we closed this period of inward attention, she described the remarkable sense of peace and connection to her mother that she felt, and voiced a clear conviction that her mother was with her still, but in an oddly spiritual/corporeal way. I would argue that my own sympathetic "channeling" of the client's experience—something that occurs for me in the great majority of sessions at cognitive, emotional, and often palpably physical levels—represents precisely the sort of *from–to* knowing that usefully orients me to the client's position and to potentially therapeutic "next steps" in our work together. In keeping with my own predilections, a recent survey of over 1000 seasoned therapists documents that those with a constructivist orientation report higher levels of self-awareness than those who work from a more rationalistic cognitive-behavioral perspective (G. J. Neimeyer et al., 2008).

In keeping with the collaborative, reflective and process-directive approach that is central to postmodern psychotherapy, the stance of the therapist is one of respectful, empathic engagement in the client's evolving narrative of self and world. The therapist does not decide what new meanings will be created, but instead assists clients in recognizing incompatible old meanings or constructs and works with them as they endeavor to find alternatives. Kelly (1955/1991) believed meanings are created and re-created through interactions between the client and the social surround (Leitner & Faidley, 2002), and that the therapist serves as a representative of the social world in therapy. For this reason, clients will often enact *transference* patterns with therapists. For Kelly transference was understood not as an inherently pathological intrusion into therapy, but rather as an inevitable outcome of human meaning making. Upon encountering the therapist for the first time, the client (like anyone else attempting to engage in a new relationship) will import into it those constructions of broadly similar relationships—as he or she sees them—in order to anticipate and "act into" the opportunities the therapist affords. For example, a client might initially anticipate that the therapist will respond like a nurturing mother, a judgmental father, a forgiving priest, a skilled physician, or a sometimes-understanding, sometimes-fickle lover. However, when constructions transferred from old relationships to new ones are too impermeable or inflexible to meet the uniqueness of the new relationship and be modified accordingly, difficulties can arise. In particular, for clients with deeply disturbed personal histories, the core of psychotherapy may consist in offering them a reparative relationship in which they are able to risk letting the therapist have access into their core understanding of self (Leitner & Faidley, 1995). The creation of this *role relationship* (in which one person attempts to construe the deepest meaning making process of another) is vital, as both client and therapist seek to establish a reverential relationship that acknowledges the uniqueness of the other. This reciprocal connection does not ordinarily imply that the therapist discloses personal *content* in the therapeutic relationship, although the disclosure of the therapist's *process responses* to the client's behavior (e.g., feeling moved by the client's courageous confrontation of a difficult issue, or feeling distanced by a client's shift toward apparently superficial content) can play a useful role in fostering client awareness and enhancing the intensity of the therapeutic connection.

Although this sort of receptive presence might seem to have mystical overtones, it can be rendered in other terms as well. Among the most adequate is Buber's evocation of an *I–Thou* relationship with the other (Buber, 1970), which presumes an essentially sacred attribution of full personhood to the other, in contrast to an *I–It* relationship, which casts the other as simply an object to be acted on for our own purposes. In more secular terms it also resonates with the cardinal role of therapeutic *empathy*, *genuineness* and *unconditional positive regard* given particular emphasis by the honored tradition of humanistic psychology, and most especially by Carl Rogers (1951). Empirical research tends to reinforce the distinctiveness of constructivist and cognitive-behavioral therapies on these dimensions, with the former being characterized by independent raters as displaying greater unconditional regard, use of open questions, and paraphrasing, whereas the latter showed more negative attitudes to the client and heavier reliance on information giving and direct guidance (Winter & Watson, 1999).

But I find that Polanyi's description adds usefully to such formulations because it highlights the necessary presence of the self in the relational knowing that is therapy, as the implicit *ground* from which our awareness is directed to the explicit *figure* of the client's words or actions. Interestingly, I think that the self of the therapist functions in a similar way for the client as well, as he or she attends from the therapist's questions or instructions to his or her own material. Thus, for both, the therapist's presence serves as a clarifying lens that brings into greater focus (inter)personal patterns and processes that are more difficult to observe in the client's private reflections.

16

## Following the affect trail

If therapist presence sets the stage for psychotherapeutic work, *process* is the medium in which the drama of therapy unfolds. Extending this metaphor, an effective therapist attends to unfolding action in the consulting room much as a director might attend to a theatrical performance, with the crucial exceptions that the director him- or herself is also an actor on the stage, and there is no script for the performance! Instead, in the improvisational theatre that is therapy, the therapist directs the process by attending to subtle signals of possible extension, elaboration or intensification of the action or emotion in promising directions, sometimes through explicit instructions or suggestions, but more commonly through her or his own responsiveness to the client's "lines" or performance.

This basic orientation to process carries several implications for the practice of therapy as a moment-to-moment transaction between two (or more) people. The first can also be stated as a guiding principle for therapy: *Follow the affect trail*. That is, significant emotion, even (or especially) when subtly present, typically defines the growing edge of the client's experiencing— the shadow of sadness that portends looming loss, the static of anxiety that announces a half-perceived threat, the spark of irritation that hints at an angry reassertion of a cherished position or boundary attendant on its sensed violation. In each instance the feeling tone underpinning the client's experience in the moment is palpably present in his or her language of gesture, proxemics, verbal, co-verbal, and nonverbal expression. Simply articulating this implicit emotion and inviting elaboration ("I notice that your jaw is trembling as you say that. What's happening for you right now?" or "If those tears could speak, what would they tell us?") is often enough to deepen the client's self-awareness, prompting symbolization of new meaning as a precondition to its further negotiation (R. A. Neimeyer, 1995a). Large-scale survey research provides evidence of this greater attention to emotion on the part of constructivist than rationalist cognitive therapists (G. J. Neimeyer et al., 2008). Likewise, close analysis of therapy sessions has established that humanistically oriented constructivist therapies tend to focus strongly on this emotional "internal" narrative process unfolding between clients and therapists, whereas cognitive behavioral therapists promote instead a more interpretive "reflexive" narrative process (Levitt & Angus, 1999).

At other points, however, emotion and other modalities (such as imagery or narrative) can be so closely inter-braided that drawing forth one automatically brings with it the other(s). An illustration of this arose for me in a recent session of therapy with a lonely client grieving the death of her father after a long lapsed relationship that recently had been rekindled. Altered by her statement that she felt like there was "a sheet of Plexiglas" between herself and others, I asked her to close her eyes and visualize that Plexiglas and her relation to it. As she did so, she described it as an "octagonal enclosure" in which she found herself alone, with others as shadowy figures passing by on the outside. When I enquired whether the enclosure had a ceiling of some sort, she replied that it did not, that it was open at the top. Visualizing the scene myself, and getting more details of her positioning in relation to the walls ("sometimes touching them, but never able to get through"), I inquired as to their height. She responded without hesitation: "Eight feet." "Hmm . . ." I wondered, "Eight feet, and eight walls in the enclosure . . . . Does the number *eight* have a special significance for you?" Immediately my client burst into tears with a slight gasp, "Yes—my father died on the 8th!" The seemingly unbreakable, unbridgeable walls in which she felt encased were the walls of her grief, cutting her off from other human contact. Elaborating the image a bit more, she described the enclosure as an aquarium and herself as the fish observing and being observed by a world beyond her reach. She eagerly accepted my suggestion as the session ended that she might write a short metaphoric story with the title *Life in the Fishbowl* as a means of extending the image, its associated feelings and meanings into our conversation the following week.

Whether emotion is given attention in its pure physical expression or in the way it resonates through a significant story or image shared in therapy, it tends to be viewed differently by constructivists than by other therapists working from a cognitive-behavioral orientation. For example, personal construct theorists interpret emotions as clues to incipient shifts in our core constructs for maintaining a sense of self and relationships (Kelly, 1955/1991), as when a client's anxiety suggests that he or she is confronting an experience without the necessary means of anticipating or making sense of it. Emotion-focused therapists working in a broadly constructivist way (Greenberg, Watson, & Lietaer, 1998) emphasize the relation between primary and secondary emotions, as in the case of a recent client whose anger and condescension toward rejecting co-workers functioned as a defensive cover for her more basic fear of isolation and abandonment—an uncomfortably familiar feeling she harbored since her childhood with distant parents. Finally, constructivists take inspiration from Mahoney's (1991) concept of emotion as a form of intuitive knowing, rather than as an irrational force to be brought into line with rational evaluations of a situation. In this way they rarely are drawn to see affect, even negative affect, as a problem to be eliminated, controlled, disputed, minimized or coped with through distraction, as might be the case in other cognitive-behavioral forms of therapy.

## Privileging experience over explanation

A corollary to the principle of following the affect trail is that *all therapeutic change is initiated in moments of experiential intensity*; all the rest is merely commentary. That is, potent interventions need not be heavy handed, but they entail ushering a client into new awareness, clarity, and possibility by engagement in an emotionally significant *experience* of something, not merely a cognitive discussion of it. My imagery work with the woman bathing in radiant connection with her mother was a case in point: once she had had this experience, consolidating it descriptively by (her) framing it as connection with her mother was relevant and useful, helping to hold the moment through "word-binding" the preverbal bodily feeling, as Kelly (1955/1991) would have said. But absent the experience, mere discussion of changed connection with her mother would have been simply abstract discourse, divested of concrete referents or novelty, and ephemeral in its effect. This strong tendency to explore and discriminate among aspects of an experience, attending to both internal and external sources of information as a prelude to their novel integration into a new perspective has been identified as a hallmark of constructivist as distinct from cognitive therapies in psychotherapy process research (Winter & Watson, 1999).

18

# Catching the wave

A further principle governing the therapeutic use of process is *timing*. Descriptively the principle is easy enough to grasp: seek the right intervention at the right moment. Pursuing something too soon, before the client's growing edge is receptive to it, will produce resistance at worst or intellectual or behavioral compliance at best, and pursuing it too late will halt the client's forward momentum and redundantly reaffirm what is already clearly enough grasped or accomplished. Both of the latter represent the cardinal constructivist "sin" of therapeutic *tracking errors* (R. A. Neimeyer & Bridges, 2003), in which the therapist loses the leading edge of the client's meaning making, like a surfer who leans too far forward on a wave's crest and is dashed beneath it or who falls too far back, loses momentum, and ends up in a lull. An example of this occurred in my otherwise effective work with a bereaved mother, Darla, who 10 minutes earlier in the session had described how other members of her family retreated in silence from the pain of their shared grief, leaving her alone in wanting to introduce her son back into the family conversation, sharing his memory and the feelings it evoked (R. A. Neimeyer, 2004). At the later therapeutic point she had moved beyond this topic to the issue of finding some new way to relate to her suffering, to "not treat it as the enemy." Still preoccupied at some level with the family's lack of openness to sharing the loss, I paused and then said, "It seems important to have people who respect your suffering, the way [your son] might have respected it." Even if the statement were true in some sense, it was poorly timed, and Darla rightly looked at me blankly, added a, "Huh . . .," with diverted eyes that suggested she was continuing to pursue her own line of thought. When I then joined her in fuller presence to her process and inquired, "What's the '*huh*'?" she readily accepted my prompting to extend the implications of her comment in strikingly fruitful directions, leading us to enact a dialogue with the suffering, personifying it in keeping with the implicit anthropomorphism with which she had spoken of the need to find a way to "work with" this seeming antagonist. Only with appropriate timing, derived from a close attunement to the client's process, can an intervention find the fertile soil it requires to germinate into fresh possibilities.

*Cultivating* a sense of timing, as opposed to simply *describing* it, is harder, however. I find that establishing presence, as discussed earlier, goes some distance in this direction, allowing me to notice clearly the gaps, leads, implications, and prospects inherent in the client's presentation in each and every speaking turn, at levels that are enacted as much as narrated. But in addition to this basic noticing I find it useful to orient to the implicit question, "What does my client need, now, in this moment, to take a further step?" Sometimes, of course, the answer is *nothing*—merely permitting a productive silence to ensue, giving the client space for further processing, in keeping with the careful psychotherapy process research of my colleagues Frankel, Levitt, Murray, Greenberg, and Angus (2006). But even this form of patient waiting is a response, as is the raised eyebrow, the knowing smile, the forward lean, the wrinkled brow that in their various ways represent an invitation to continue or say more. Like the more obvious interventions of questions, prompts or instructions, all of these require an intuitive read of their appropriateness in the present moment with and for the client. I find Jung's definition apt here: "the intuitive process is neither one of sense-perception nor of thinking, nor yet of feeling . . . [but rather] is one of the basic functions of the psyche, namely *perception of the possibilities inherent in a situation*" (Jung, 1971). Therapy is most effective when it intuitively seeks, finds, and grafts onto this emergent sense of possibility. The finding that constructivist therapists acknowledge greater openness to experience than their more rationalistic cognitive colleagues (G. J. Neimeyer et al., 2008) accords with this process orientation.

19

# Harnessing the power of the poetic

A further principle of process might be phrased as: *Speak poetically, rather than prosaically, for maximum impact.*[2] Of course, much of therapeutic discourse is necessarily practical, descriptive and representational—staying close to the language of everyday life (and of the client) in order to intelligibly engage the mundane realities of the client's life world. But a therapy that does not at least occasionally lift above this to highlight or offer a less literal, but richly imagistic depiction of the client's problem, position or possibilities fails in Kelly's (1977) basic charge to *transcend the obvious*, that is, not merely to map current realities, but rather to foster their transformation by casting them in fresh and figurative terms. Listening to Kelly's tapes of therapy with a formal and isolated client during my graduate school years, I was struck by his frequent use of highly poetic and evocative language, as when he would confront the client with a comment like, "And so here is the man, the man in the hollow sphere . . . ," as a prompt for deepening beyond the litany of weekly complaints that kept the client fixed in his present unsatisfying relational patterns.

Although the therapist's use of poetically vivid formulations can often be powerful in this sense, they can also fail if they do not meet the twin tests of following the client's affect trail and being well timed, as elaborated earlier. An antidote for this over-eagerness on the part of the therapist is to attend to the *quality*

2 In recent years I have been taking myself more literally in this respect, out of the therapy room as well as in it. One result is *Rainbow in the Stone* (R. A. Neimeyer, 2006b), a collection of poems that often arise from my clinical contact with clients, as well as with the broader world.

*terms* resident in the client's speech,[3] those turns of phrase that reveal his or her position with special clarity and precision. Such terms are typically signaled in any or all of three modalities: the client's use of metaphor, co-verbal inflection (as through variations in prosody or intensity of speech), or nonverbal underscoring by facial expression or gesture. An example arose in my therapy with Susan, who was speaking of the unfamiliar sense of confidence she mustered as she served as family caregiver to her dying mother. In response to my question of how her mother responded to this self-presentation, she acknowledged that her "mom had a hard time accepting, umm . . . this new *façade* of me." Allowing her to finish her elaboration of her new strength, I then returned to the quality term in her statement, signaled by both vocal emphasis and by its highly figurative quality. I began, "A moment ago, you said your mother had a difficult time accepting this new *façade* of you . . . ," when she interrupted, "Did I use that word, *façade*?" I assured her she did, and suggested that the word implied a kind of *mask*, something that was only *surface deep*. She replied, "That's true, that's true . . . . It was like a new . . . *garment*. But now it's becoming more comfortable" (moving her shoulders and arms, as if breaking in a new jacket). We went on to acknowledge explicitly how the mantle of confidence was now feeling more like *her* and to explore the validation she had subsequently received for this enduring strength from her strongly independent sister and daughters. Subtle attention to a client's personal descriptors of an experience as a way of entering his or her internal frame of reference has been found to distinguish constructivist therapies from their cognitive-behavioral cousins in research on therapy process (Winter & Watson, 1999).

Striking support for the power of metaphor in therapy has been provided by Martin (1994), who documents the much

---

3 I owe this term to my colleague Sandy Woolum, a practicing therapist and trainer in Duluth, Minnesota.

higher degree to which clients recall their therapists' interventions a few months later when these are phrased in figuratively rich terms, often arising from or contributing to the co-construction of metaphors first implicitly introduced by a client. As he further notes, these are the very quality terms the client ultimately uses to challenge and change his or her theory of the problem and the self that sustains it. Thus, if therapy is understood as a form of *rhetoric*, that is, an artful use of language to achieve practical ends, it is clear that an attention to and use of poetic and figurative speech plays an important part in the process.

20

# Seeking sufficient structure

Finally, of the triad of therapeutic practices outlined here, procedure is the most concrete. Whereas *presence* places the alert and responsive therapist fully in an intersubjective field shared with the client, and attention to *process* characterizes their subtly shifting ongoing communication, concrete therapeutic *procedures* address specific goals and draw upon identifiable change strategies. Here I will address some of the basic procedural parameters of constructivist therapy, and then illustrate some of its distinctive techniques for prompting therapeutic reflection and change.

There is no preferred timetable for therapy that characterizes all postmodern practice. Several contemporary constructivist therapists have followed Kelly's lead in advocating that therapy be as efficient as possible, as the 1 to 6 sessions that characterize coherence therapy illustrate (Ecker & Hulley, 1996). On the other hand, some constructivist counselors adopt the model of therapy as "intermittent long-term consultation," in which the therapist remains available as a guide or "fellow traveler" from time to time, as the client encounters unexpected detours or impasses along life's journey (Mahoney, 1991). Some developmentally oriented constructivist therapists even plan intensive, long-term therapies that can span years of work, seeking to reveal and restructure the client's basic affective stance in intimate relationships (Arciero & Guidano, 2000; Guidano, 1995). The timing of sessions is similarly variable. Kelly's (1955/ 1991) fixed-role therapy typically involves multiple sessions of practice and processing across a two- or three-week period as clients confront the challenge of enacting new roles or identities in their social world, whereas family therapies that adopt a postmodern emphasis often are conducted on a monthly basis, allowing members time to integrate the changes provoked by sessions in the weeks between (Procter, 1987). As these examples imply, *who* attends sessions can be as variable as *when* they do so, with many postmodern practitioners moving smoothly from an individual to a relational focus and back again, with shifting participation within a given therapy in keeping with immediately relevant goals (Efran, Lukens, & Lukens, 1990). Likewise, innovative group therapy formats, such as the Interpersonal Transaction Group (R. A. Neimeyer, 1988) and Multiple Self Awareness Group (Sewell, Baldwin, & Moes, 1998), systematically promote alternating engagement in individual or dyadic reflection, followed by whole-group processing or enactments based on the results of this personal exploration. Accordingly, the degree of structure within sessions varies widely, although a general precept of seeking minimum sufficient structure to serve therapeutic goals is typically advocated. This tendency toward greater flexibility as opposed to rigidity in structuring sessions and breadth versus narrowness of focus in therapy has been found to distinguish constructivist from rationalist cognitive therapists (G. J. Neimeyer et al., 2008).

## Tracking evolving goals

Therapeutic objectives in postmodern therapies are rarely imposed by the therapist and, indeed, are often imprecisely understood by even the client prior to engagement in the therapeutic process. What is typically clear to both is that the client is in some form of distress; something about the client's means of engaging the social world is painful, and perhaps recurrently so. But aside from alleviating this distress, the implications of the initial complaint for their work together will often require further elaboration, during which the problem is likely to undergo change and redefinition (Kelly, 1955/1991). Thus, in sharp contrast to therapeutic perspectives that emphasize the importance of establishing clearly defined target goals from the outset of therapy, postmodern perspectives typically seek to foster a sense of "spaciousness" in the therapeutic hour, a minimally structured encounter in which the initially vague "felt sense" of the problem can be carefully articulated in a way that yields greater clarity and direction (Gendlin, 1996).

But the general distrust of agenda-driven sessions in no way suggests that constructivist therapies are wandering, inefficient, or directionless. On the contrary, as suggested above, the therapist is at every moment of therapeutic contact seeking to focus on precisely that "growing edge" of the client's feelings, concerns, understanding, or preparedness for action that is most ready for attention and extension. For example, this stance might find expression in therapist inquiries at the start of a session like, "*What do you feel ready to accomplish today?*" "*What would you like this session to do for you?*" or "*What has become clearer for you since the last time we met?*" In addition, it suggests the relevance of looking for specific "markers" of implicit "tasks" that clients are ready to undertake in just this moment of therapy (Greenberg, Elliott, & Rice, 1993), such as the "unfinished business" with her father that suggested the relevance of an imaginal two-chair dialogue in the case of Joanne with which this book opened. Such an approach uses the moment-to-moment interaction between client and therapist as the surest and most efficient guide to identifying *process goals* of immediate relevance to the therapy, rather than generically relevant agendas for gross classes of problems (e.g., depression, social anxiety) or clients (e.g., "borderlines," trauma survivors). Thus, in the terms of Mahoney (1988), postmodern therapies are less "teleological"—oriented toward some pre-envisioned objective—than they are "teleonomic"—displaying meaningful evolution across time, even though the final outcome cannot be forecast in advance.

# Fostering client reflexivity

At an abstract level, however, postmodern therapies can be said to have certain *outcome goals*, which include enhancing client reflexivity, or self-awareness and capacity for self-change (Rennie, 1992); relational responsiveness and openness to others at core levels (Leitner, 1995); empowerment or a sense of "voice" in their lives (Brown, 2000b); and the enactment and social affirmation of a preferred self-narrative (Eron & Lund, 1996).

In general, postmodern psychotherapy, like many humanistic approaches, construes change as arising largely from the client's meaning-making capabilities (Bohart & Tallman, 1999). Although new possibilities are brought forth in the dialogic relationship between the client and the therapist, it is client activity and insight that ultimately produce lasting life adaptations. Thus, therapist designs and interventions have only an instigating role as curative factors, serving mainly to highlight client resources (mal)adaptive core meaning-making processes, and modes of relating that have lost their utility. As such, specific techniques are primarily useful in that they help to elaborate personal meaning-making activities of the client, rather than producing change in and of themselves.

The client reflexivity regarding problematic constructions or life narratives that is valued by most postmodern therapists is sometimes, but by no means routinely, supported by historical interpretations of how those patterns came into existence in formative experiences in the client's life. However, the "interpretation" that is crucial here is rarely that of the therapist— instead, it is the meaning attributed to such patterns by the client that triggers insight and possible behavior change.

Therapists working within such an understanding therefore typically avoid highly interpretive interactions with clients and instead concentrate on experiential interventions (as illustrated in case examples elsewhere in this book) that assist the client in encountering in a vivid way those circumstances that contributed to their adoption of a self-limiting pattern that has been perpetuated in current situations. Ultimately, in keeping with constructivist metatheory, the interpretations placed on the client's life experiences need not be *literally* true (such as determining whether a parent was or was not in fact abusive), so long as they correspond to the *emotional* truth of the client (Ecker & Hulley, 1996) and carry helpful implications for approaching the future in a new way (Kelly, 1969). A similar orientation to the "narrative truth" rather than the "historical truth" of the client's experience is evident in constructivist variations of contemporary psychodynamic therapy (Spence, 1982).

If there are "skills" that are relevant to the promotion of self-change in postmodern therapies, they would focus primarily on the client's abilities to explore the subtle interbraiding of personal and social meaning making, the capacity to symbolize, articulate, and renegotiate those constructions of self and world that promote or impede adaptation to shifting life experiences (R. A. Neimeyer, 1995a). In this sense, an ultimate goal of constructivist psychotherapies is helping clients become *connoisseurs of their experience*, leaving them better positioned to grasp the entailments of their current self-narratives and to craft and perform new ones.

# 23

# Befriending the resistance

In most cognitive-behavioral forms of therapy, as in traditional psychotherapy generally, client resistance to the "work" of therapy tends to be viewed negatively, in terms of the client's motivational deficit, noncompliance, motivated avoidance of something difficult or painful, or reactance against therapist control. Accordingly, therapists apply a whole range of techniques to overcome this impediment to psychotherapeutic progress, ranging from psychoeducation, through behavioral activation and increasing the power of reinforcement contingencies to allowing clients to choose from a broader menu of homework assignments.

In contrast, postmodern psychotherapists tend to view resistance as either an *ambivalent choice* or as a necessary form of *self-protection*, each of which calls for rather different responses on the part of the therapist (Frankel & Levitt, 2006). For example, personal construct theorists see a client's reluctance to change as an adaptive response to the threat of change to core ways of understanding the world (Kelly, 1955/1991). It is for this reason that specialized assessment techniques have been devised to identify constructs that are likely to be resistant to modification (see above) and that approaches like fixed-role therapy mitigate the threat of change by allowing clients to wear the protective mask of "make believe" as they experiment with new roles that do not contradict their previous constructions of self and others.

In fact, resistance is usually more apparent when core, identity-defining constructs are being challenged, and, as such, it can provide a window into the symptom-maintaining processes of the client. For example, as described below, Ecker and

Hulley's (2008) coherence therapy welcomes the resistance that often arises when therapists ask clients to visualize themselves in a familiar problem situation but without resorting to the usual symptomatic behavior. In such instances, clients often find themselves unable to step into a symptom-free position, even in their imagination, allowing the therapist to interview them directly about what makes it essential to retain the consciously problematic, but unconsciously essential, symptomatic way of being.

From a rather different standpoint, narrative therapists (White & Epston, 1990) respond to clients' struggles in overcoming a problematic pattern by *externalizing the problem* (as illustrated below) and then joining with clients in analyzing its "real effects" on their lives, sometimes inviting them to speak as if they were the dominant problem (e.g., alcohol, anxiety) in order to describe clearly and vividly its "relationship" to the clients over time, and in the course of doing so, mount resistance against the resistance (e.g., R. A. Neimeyer, 2006a). "Befriending" or "dialoging" with the resistance in this way, rather than merely interpreting it or seeking compliance with therapist requests, can thereby lead to greater therapeutic progress. Frankel and Levitt (2006) provide a thorough discussion of conceptualizations of and strategic responses to client resistance from the standpoint of several forms of post-modern, constructivist psychotherapy.

# 24

## Considering homework

As suggested by my discussion of therapeutic structure, goal-setting, and specific procedures such as those described under both assessment and psychotherapy, between-session activities are considered a useful adjunct to some, but by no means all, forms of postmodern practice. When they occur, they are as likely to stem from the initiative of the client as from the explicit assignment of the therapist, although a wide range of therapist-suggested assignments that grow organically from the session may also be used. The latter can range in complexity from the pro-symptom position (PSP) note task used in coherence therapy to detailed assignments to draft a "character sketch" of oneself as if one were the lead protagonist of a book or film or to enact a hypothetical role in the social world, as in Kelly's (1955/1991) fixed-role therapy. Although several such tasks have been devised and are used with some frequency by constructivists (see R. A. Neimeyer & Winter, 2006, for a toolbox of such methods with clinical examples), in general constructivist therapy is less prescriptive in this regard than other forms of cognitive therapy, for which various forms of self-monitoring and explicit efforts at behavior modification are considered central mechanisms of change (Kazantzis & L'Abate, 2006). The general skepticism about the heavy use of therapist-assigned homework among postmodern practitioners reflects their conviction that change emerges more as a result of client activity than therapist design (Bohart & Tallman, 1999), and hence should not typically be engineered by a high level of therapist prescriptions.

25

# Articulating the pro-symptom position

As noted by Kelly (1955/1991), constructivist therapies tend to be "technically eclectic but theoretically consistent," promoting the use of diverse change strategies within an integrative but evolving understanding of each case. To illustrate the diversity of these methods, I will focus on two somewhat complementary approaches that derive from a more individualistic constructivist model and a more culturally oriented social constructionist model, respectively, each of which makes a contribution to the detailed case study with which this book concludes.

*Coherence therapy* (Ecker & Hulley, 2008), originally termed Depth-Oriented Brief Therapy or DOBT (Ecker & Hulley, 1996), aims to produce swift change by revealing and transforming those initially unconscious constructions of reality that make the client's problem vitally necessary to maintain, despite the very real suffering it causes. This central assumption of *symptom coherence* posits that, far from reflecting a *disorder*, the symptom or problem a client presents actually reflects a hidden *order*, in the sense that it arises from the activation of specific personal constructs scaffolding the client's perception of the concrete situation, the self, and the social world. The methodology of the approach consists of actively guiding clients to encounter these very constructs in vividly experiential ways as a precondition to their integration and transformation.

Typically clients begin therapy consciously identified with an *anti-symptom position*, in which they view the symptom (e.g., depression, unassertiveness, procrastination, cycles of arguing with a partner) as an unnecessary impediment in their lives. In traditional cognitive-behavioral therapies the counselor and client work together against the problem, in an attempt to counteract it directly through the application of specific techniques (e.g., behavioral activation, cognitive restructuring) or to develop compensatory coping skills for managing it. In contrast, in coherence therapy the counselor works experientially with the client to identify the *emotional truth* of the symptom— the unconscious *pro-symptom position* that makes the symptom vitally necessary to maintain. Only by fully integrating this position into conscious awareness can the client either recognize that it no longer has relevance to his or her life by juxtaposing it with other living knowledge or, alternatively, acknowledge its adaptive value in the present and realign goals so that the "symptom" becomes a *choice*, rather than a problem. Thus, coherence therapy represents a deep implementation of the personal-agentic premises of the epigenetic framework, by bringing to life the hidden agency at the root of symptom production.

There are four main features of successful coherence therapy (Ecker & Hulley, 2000). First, the therapist needs to engage and validate empathically the very real suffering of the client in relation to the symptom; the assumption that the problem serves deep purposes does not in itself mitigate the pain it causes the client and significant others. Second, the unconscious pro-symptom position that requires the symptom needs to be discovered *experientially* by the client, prompted by any of several forms of *radical questioning* by the therapist; it is not a matter of being offered an intellectual "insight" by a clever or all-knowing therapist. Third, it is vital to fully integrate the specific themes and purposes of that emotional reality into the consciousness of the client, sometimes underscoring them through a self-awareness task at the end of the session, as in the case vignette that follows. Fourth, and finally, there is the transformation of previous meaning making to be more congruent with the main themes and purposes underlying the presenting symptomatology. Because this approach to therapy goes deeply into core issues from the very first session, change is typically rapid, with a slowing of therapy more often owing to therapist timidity than to client resistance.

My therapy with Nora, a 40-year-old executive, illustrates this methodology. Nora was referred to me by her psychiatrist for "cognitive therapy" to help her deal with her "hair trigger anger," which was especially salient in relation to her husband of eight years, Brian. In her opening statement Nora readily conceded that despite her being "highly functional" in her work life, she was easily provoked to rage at her husband, something that raised increasing concern for her now that she and Brian had a small child whom she wanted to protect from witnessing such outbursts. Moreover, Nora was genuinely perplexed by this behavior, as she denied any legitimate reason for her anger (e.g., any abuse or wrong doing on Brian's part or suspicion of his having an affair, or drug use or significant drinking on the part of either that would disinhibit such displays of temper). No stranger to therapy, Nora was eager to work with me using various self-control strategies, although a two-year effort to do so with a competent cognitive-behavior therapist had brought only ephemeral relief, and a subsequent course of couples therapy had similarly fleeting effects. Alerted to the failure of these counteractive approaches that sought to curb or nullify the symptom through rational disputation, couples contracting and similar procedures, I decided instead to begin by eliciting a concrete recent example of Nora's escalation. She had no trouble honestly acknowledging several such instances in the past week, in which she "attacked" Brian for "wastefully" hiring a gardener, despite their comfortable six-figure income, "blasted" him with names like "idiot" and various profanities for leaving the water running in the sink, and other apparently minor transgressions. For his part, Brian would retaliate, but rarely to the point of "winning," and would usually slink away to "lick his wounds."

From an *anti-symptom position*, Nora was genuinely pained and embarrassed by these altercations, and consciously "wanted to learn to respect Brian, rather than constantly pick at him." I therefore used the technique of *symptom deprivation*, not as a form of "cognitive rehearsal" for behavior change, but as a way of encountering the part of her that resisted this apparently idyllic state of affairs. Asking her to close her eyes, I asked her to visualize an image of herself and Brian at home together, perhaps reading and chatting or doing a simple household chore together amicably, and then to simply say to herself, "This is lovely. I feel just fine about this." Within seconds Nora's brow furrowed, and frowning, she acknowledged quietly, "My immediate 'brain' was to find something to criticize about him . . . . The pressure to do it just builds . . . . It's like we don't have anything to talk about if we're not fighting." Sensing the initial emergence of a previously hidden pro-symptom position, I picked up a Post-It note and wrote on it, "The truth is that I *need* to find something to criticize about Brian to relieve my tension. If not, we would have nothing to say to each other. The terms of our attachment require argumentation." Handing her this *overt statement* in the form of the note, I asked her to read it slowly aloud, allowing herself to edit it as needed to make it emotionally true for her. She did so pensively and nodded her head slowly, then looked up and said, "Yeah, I guess that's *right*." Nora then quickly associated to her father's "rageful anger," which she described as the "sad legacy" of a life she otherwise respected and emulated. "All my life," she said, had been, "one long battle to stop this, to find other ways to connect." I therefore inscribed a second, shorter note, which she read aloud: "But in the end, I'd rather be sad and angry than disconnected." Again, she responded soberly, "That's true." Sensing there was more emotional truth to be mined from this vein of association, I asked her to close her eyes and simply note what happened when she invited herself to complete the sentence, "If I didn't fight with and criticize Brian, then I'd . . . ." Nora's response surprised us both, as she looked puzzled and said, "Be afraid." "Of . . . ?" I prompted, but nothing came.

Trying a different, less verbal angle of approach, I invited Nora to simply scan her body, looking for the site where she felt the fear most keenly. After a few moments, she gestured toward her forehead and said, "Initially, it was in my head, like a pain in front, and on the left side of my face . . . but then it was also *here*" [forming parentheses with her hands at the level of her abdomen]. I waited a moment, then asked quietly, "Does that feeling in your abdomen have a color or form?" It did, she replied, something *dark* and *hard*. Requesting that she tell me more about that, Nora continued by describing it as a *crescent* shape, like a "boundary, a kind of limit . . . something that stops anything that tries to expand past it." After pausing a few moments, I asked her to imagine that boundary opening just slightly, and to notice if there was any emotional change. Immediately she had an image of the boundary dissolving, and with it came a flood of uncertainty, sadness and tears, as she stammered, "I just don't know what I'd replace that with." In quick succession Nora then associated to her "worry about the irretrievable damage" she'd done to her relationship with Brian, and then again growing quiet, added uncertainly, "Something about the *tragedy of my father's anger* comes into this, and that makes me very sad." I concluded by writing an additional rendition of her emerging pro-symptom position, as follows:

> At one level, my anger protects me from: (a) the uncertainty of what change would mean; (b) needing to find a replacement for my familiar rage; (c) the guilt of how I have scarred my marriage; and (d) the sadness and grief of my family tragedy. As much as my anger troubles and embarrasses me, the truth is that I desperately need the shield that it provides.

Reading this, Nora nodded sadly and elaborated briefly on how she was indeed, "her father's daughter," manifesting his same success and his same failures. I closed our first session by asking her to simply place the Post-It notes with her pro-symptom positions (PSPs) in the daily agenda she had brought with her to the session to schedule our next appointment, and make a point of reading these at least daily—especially before going home to spend time with Brian—with no attempt whatsoever to change these seemingly automatic patterns. Instead, the goal was simply to recognize consciously some of the vital purposes served by her anger at him, rather than to act on them habitually. Intrigued, she agreed, and closed by sharing the reaction that she found this first session surprisingly "powerful, refreshing, and deep." We scheduled a second session for seven days later.

Returning the next week, Nora opened the session by noting, "So many synapses connected as I drove away from our session. It was a real moment of clarity." As requested, she had read her PSPs daily, even sticking them to her bathroom mirror to make them more unavoidable. Doing so, she had several additional revelations, beginning with how Brian sometimes uncomfortably mirrored his own father's behavior, which was more loud and boorish than that of her "brilliant," urbane parents. Holding her PSPs consciously in mind, she sidestepped her usual defensive response of anger and allowed herself to feel the fear beneath it. As we explored this fear in session she first shared her concern that Brian, like his father, was merely unintelligent, a "big talker," but noted immediately that "that could be more surface." What came next was more self-relevant: the fear that if Brian were "nothing special," then she wasn't either. What followed was *serial accessing* of several further PSPs, eventuating in a tearful articulation of her own crushingly low self-esteem, which took the form of her acknowledging how she viciously shouted, "I hate you!" and, "Fuck you!" at herself when she encountered her own weaknesses and foibles. As Nora noted, "So much of my identity is wrapped up in my success at work. The self-hatred comes from when I make mistakes, from when I'm immature, from my need to have 'position.' I'm just flooded with these little memories." It soon followed that only by relentlessly pushing Brian to be "superior" could she maintain the illusion that she was too. We concluded the session by formulating and asking her to read two more overt statements of the newly emerging PSPs:

When I am honest with myself, I realize that my anger at Brian is necessary to mask my anger at myself. The truth is that at some level I hate myself for my immaturity and need for position, and this floods me with self-contempt.

I can't let myself be "normal," and so I can't let Brian be "normal" either. I fear that if Brian is just normal, then that means that I am too, and that wouldn't be okay in my family.

As these and similar PSPs were consciously integrated, Nora found that their hold on her continued to loosen, and she reported the surprising new awareness that she and Brian actually had a capacity to relate to one another with far less acrimony without losing their connection. Similarly, she found herself more comfortable assuming a "one down" position with her staff, permitting them to take the lead on projects without her micromanagement. Although she continued to contend with self-criticism, she was able to put this into words and "own" it, rather than "throwing it like a live hand grenade in the direction of others." At the time of this writing, our work seems to be moving quickly toward family-of-origin patterns that "installed" her low self-esteem as a paradoxical pattern of adaptation, using the same coherence-based methods that have taken much of the "steam" out of the PSPs she first articulated in our early sessions. Interestingly, Ecker and Toomey (2008) have begun to link this methodology for experientially activating and then deactivating such pro-symptom configurations to novel findings in cognitive neuroscience that suggest that long-established limbic connections can indeed be "unlearned," not merely extinguished via competing associations as assumed by traditional learning theory. If these conceptual bridges were validated by subsequent research, this would link the personal-agentic work of coherence therapy with bio-genetic mechanisms of change at subcortical levels, opening an exciting horizon for the further development of psychotherapy.

# Re-authoring the self-narrative

Spanning the cultural-linguistic, dyadic-relational, and personal-agentic levels of the epigenetic model, narrative therapy seeks to reveal the narrow societal prescriptions and assumptions that constrain people's ability to recognize the options open to them (Winslade & Monk, 2001). Because problematic identities are inevitably constructed in social contexts and sustained in repetitive interactions between people, it is these very patterns or *dominant narratives* that become the initial focus of therapeutic attention in this approach, as the therapist works with the client to make more visible the influence of the problem-saturated story in his or her life. Using *curious questions*, the therapist then helps the client "deconstruct" the dominant account of his or her problem and begin to recognize his or her influence on the problem itself. By gradually noticing, historicizing, documenting, and circulating the client's steps toward a preferred story of life and relationships, the therapist helps him or her consolidate an alternative self-narrative, one more rich in possibility (White & Epston, 1990).

Like feminist therapists, narrative therapists are especially vigilant in detecting the role of cultural discourses that reinforce problematic identities or relational practices, such as the prescriptions for acceptable appearance that engender anorexic behaviors among young women, or discourses of personal entitlement that induce couples into conflict-saturated exchanges in divorce mediation contexts. By first *externalizing* these discursive patterns, the therapist helps clients recognize that *they* are not the problem but that the *problem* is the problem and that they can take an active role in resisting its influence.

The typical steps entailed in this narrative approach can be illustrated by the case of David, a young man in his early twenties, who struggled with depression to such an extent that he dropped out of school although he was a capable student; was becoming estranged from his family; and was beginning to call in sick consistently to his place of employment. When he began to isolate himself in his room and make indirect allusions to suicide, his parents pressed him to seek therapy with me.

Accompanied to his first therapy session by his father, David immediately conveyed the impression of a young man in torment, whose obvious suffering elicited helpless expressions of concern by his father, expressions that David consistently rebuffed. I therefore focused principally on David, asking his permission to interview him in more detail about the problem while his father remained in the room as a silent witness. David readily agreed. As David recounted the story of his struggle with the problem in outline form, I asked him, "What would you call this problem that seems to have enveloped your life and obscured your future?" David's immediate answer, "A black fog," was more evocative than the clinical term "depression," and provided a first approximation to naming the problem as something that seemed to have taken on a life of its own over the last several years. Continuing this *externalizing conversation*, I asked David to say more about the history of the problem, prompting him occasionally with questions such as, "When did this black fog first creep into your life?" "What did the landscape of your life look like before it arrived?" and "When did you first notice it darkening your perception of the world?" David responded that the fog made its first appearance when he was in high school, when the promise of a brilliant athletic career began to dim, despite his father and coach's faith in his abilities. I gradually shifted toward mapping the "real effects" of the fog in his life through the use of *relative influence questioning*: "What effect would you say the fog has had on your view of yourself and your abilities?" "What plans does the fog have for your educational and occupational future?" "To what extent has the fog seeped into your home life?" and "Who in the family seems to be most lost in the fog with you?" David responded to these inquiries with increasing animation, noting how "different" they felt from the internalizing conversations with other professionals that implicitly lodged the problem *inside* him, in terms of cognitive distortions, behavioral deficits, and biochemical imbalances. As a result of this changed perspective, he began to recognize the impact the problem had had on his darkening view of himself and how it also was making him and his family more and more "invisible" to one another. With these effects in full view, David was ripe for considering questions about *his* influence on the *problem*, using both metaphors implicit in his description of the problem and derived from his athletic background: "What actions have you taken to try to cut through the fog?" "Are there times that you have been able to score points against it, even when you feel like the underdog?" "Are there others who seem to be playing on your team at those times?" "Who in your life is most convinced that you can make a comeback?" Gradually, David began to identify a handful of *unique outcomes* (White & Epston, 1990), "sparkling moments" in which he was able to resist the influence of the dominant narrative of depression. As he did so, he touchingly reached out to his father in response to the questions regarding valued teammates, bringing tears to the eyes of each of us. In our next session David brought me a remarkable personal journal that he was writing, entitled "Lost in the Fog: A Portrait of Depression." As he began to make tangible gains in returning to work and opening to conversations with family members—both in extended family therapy sessions and in his daily life—we began to historicize this *preferred story* of David as someone who was resilient and resourceful, who was increasingly able to glimpse the outlines of a more satisfying future through the thinning fog of his depression. Selected readings, such as Parker Palmer's (2000) *Let Your Life Speak: Listening to the Voice of Vocation*, offered David alternative and more affirmative understandings of his years of impasse and career indecision, a general narrative frame that he readily appropriated and extended in personal directions. With his family's assent, David expressed confidence in his ability to continue to resist depression's influence after six sessions of therapy, and follow-up contact suggested that he continued to make positive strides several months later. Detailed procedures for conducting narrative therapy have been drafted for a great diversity of problems, ranging from conflict mediation (Winslade & Monk, 2001) to stuttering (DiLollo, Neimeyer, & Manning, 2002), and for both children (Freeman, Epston, & Lobovits, 1997) and adults (Monk, Winslade, Crocket, & Epston, 1996). Recent qualitative research has also begun to identify distinct categories of *innovative moments* in which a client's self-narrative pivots toward change in the therapeutic dialogue, whose use in process-outcome research is helping to map the contours of narrative therapy and suggest helpful conversational practices for a wide range of clients (Gonçalves, Matos, & Santos, in press).

27

# Celebrating termination

Finally, no discussion of the therapeutic process would be complete without a discussion of *termination*. In postmodern perspectives such as narrative therapy, termination is a mutually decided upon process that is viewed as a graduation or a rite of passage (Epston & White, 1995) to a preferred identity, a transition that is in itself therapeutic. Consolidating gains made over the course of therapy can be accomplished through the use of a variety of questions, such as the following:

- If you were to write a manual for how to overcome the problem you've just conquered, what sort of ideas would it include? What personal and relationship qualities allowed you to identify this know-how and put it to use? How could you keep this knowledge alive in your own life in the future?
- If someone else consulted me for a problem like the one that once dominated your life, what advice might you offer about how to overcome its influence? Could you as a veteran of this battle write a letter of encouragement that I might share with such a person?
- What might we have seen in your previous life that would have tipped us off to your ability to break free of the problem now?
- What has this experience taught you about the kind of person you are and the kind of life story you want to live in the future?
- How would the knowledge you now have about yourself influence your next step forward? What would the person

you will be a few years from now have to say to the person who is sitting here today about what is possible in his life?
- Now that you have reached this point of graduation into a different kind of life, who else should know about it? What difference do you think it would make in their attitude toward you if they had this news?

Such questions can also be augmented by any of a number of creative documents offered by the therapist to acknowledge this passage (e.g., "Declarations of Independence" from the problem, "Certificates of Special Knowledge" recognizing major insights, or diplomas signaling graduation from therapy). Final sessions can also be planned as ritual or celebratory occasions in which key support figures in the individual's life might be invited to a social occasion that honors the client's achievements (White & Epston, 1990). Thus, far from traditional conceptions of termination as loss of a special relationship with the therapist or a hazardous transition in the generalization of therapist-taught skills, the completion of therapy can itself help empower the client in pursuing a more satisfying life narrative in the future.

28

# Evaluating whether psychotropic medication is part of the solution, or part of the problem

To a greater extent than most cognitive therapists, constructivist psychologists tend to express suspicion about the increasing reliance on psychotropic medication as a commercially advertised "quick fix" for everything from the blues to social anxiety. Moreover, many fear that pharmacotherapy can compete with psychotherapy, perhaps stripping away the motivation for more deep-going changes in life, while at the same time risking reinforcing a biological attribution for existential, personal, or relational difficulties. The result is a general hostility to the medical model of psychological distress, with its attendant implication that the problems clients bring to therapy can be substantially assuaged by the appropriate prescription.

Although I am sympathetic to all of these concerns, my own response to the question of medication is more pragmatic: I think it's often helpful, except when it's not! At any given time, 15–20% of my clients are taking medication (often having been referred to me in the first place by their psychiatrists), and the majority of them report being helped by it. In my view, nothing in this practice is incompatible with a constructivist therapy. What is inimical is considering pharmacotherapy as a substitute for self-understanding, reflexivity, self-change, resistance against oppressive circumstances and problem resolution at more psychosocial levels. Medication can sometimes give clients the wherewithal to engage life differently, but pharmacotherapy by itself rarely resolves the intricate ways in which clients get "stuck" in life. Too often, people are still living in unsatisfying relationships, still falling short of who they think they could be, and still living lives that are invisibly bound by the constraints of unexamined assumptions. The latter problems are not resolved by medication, though medication may help achieve the clarity needed to address them. Of course, some pharmacotherapy also poses high risk, such as the tendency of anti-anxiety drugs to promote addiction or to foster avoidance of the problems that clients need to engage. This in itself, however, is not a principled indictment of all psychotropic medication.

In keeping with the epigenetic model, this suggests that it can be helpful to construe human problems in biological as well as psychosocial terms. But constructivists rarely assume that the people who consult them do so because of an insufficiency in neurotransmission. Human beings also confront impasses in the way they language their lives, in how they live and construct problems in connection with themselves and others, and in the way that social life itself produces problems from which therapy is one but not the only exit. In other words, people may have difficulties that can be addressed biologically, but that does not exhaust the realm of human problems.

Ultimately, constructivists do not conceptualize problems as having either biological causes or social causes or personal, family, legal or cultural origins. Instead, like Kelly (1955/1991), they tend to view all of these domains—biology, psychology, family studies, sociology, law—as simply explanatory systems that have partial, but incomplete relevance to a much more holistic process that is called being human. Thus, at different times it is helpful to look at human difficulties from each of these vantage points, but the problems themselves have no allegiance to any one of these explanatory systems.

Therapists animated by a social constructionist spirit sometimes adopt a similar blend of skepticism and pragmatism regarding the utility of medication in psychological treatment. For instance, the work of Seikkula and his colleagues in Finland with families experiencing the psychotic deterioration of one of their members relies principally upon the use of "open dialogue," in which integrated teams of professionals work intensively with families in their homes to foster deep-going discussions of the significance of the distressing symptoms, with full participation of the identified patient (Seikkula, Alakare, & Aaltonen, 2001a). In this work, the psychotic reactions are viewed as attempts to make sense of traumatic or difficult life events, which need to be understood rather than simply pharmacologically controlled. However, in approximately 25% of cases neuroleptic medication was deemed appropriate in order to make the patient's coherent participation in the dialogue process possible. Nonetheless, outcome data suggested that pharmacotherapy was actually associated with *poorer* outcome in most cases; indeed, of the 61% of "good outcome" cases, less that 20% had been prescribed anti-psychotic medication, whereas over 50% of "poor outcome" cases had been medicated (Seikkula, Alakare, & Aaltonen, 2001b). Although no causal inference can be drawn from this non-randomized study, it does underscore both the willingness of postmodern, social constructionist therapists to consider medication, and the importance of not assuming that adjunctive pharmacotherapy ensures treatment effectiveness.

# 29

# Situating constructivist therapy in the wider world

Every approach to psychotherapy, constructivism included, necessarily finds its place in a distinctive historical, cultural, and professional context, which presents it with both challenges and opportunities. In the present case, I will focus on a handful of the issues faced by contemporary constructivism and under-score, where appropriate, features that distinguish it from its cognitive-behavioral alternatives. These include the diversity of constructivist practice, distinctive features of postmodern ethics, and the research base of this perspective.

One of the great strengths of this orientation is its inter-nationality, with active research and practice groups animated by postmodern ideas literally spanning the globe, from the USA, Canada and the United Kingdom to Australia and New Zealand. Nor is the theory group confined principally to English-speaking countries, as innovative developments are burgeoning in such countries as Germany, Italy, Norway, Sweden, Finland, Portugal, Brazil, Serbia, and the Netherlands. The Hispanic world is particularly "constructivized," with numerous training centers being found in Spain, Argentina, Chile, and Mexico. Even major university-based training centers in Asian countries—especially China and Japan—are being attracted to constructivist models of practice, perhaps because of their inherent respect for different cultural and philosophic systems. The result is a rich blending of traditions, many of which draw inspiration from indigenous cultures like the Maori of New Zealand, whose communal practices of respectful negotiation and conflict resolution can be read between the lines of many narrative approaches to therapy and mediation (White

& Epston, 1990; Winslade & Monk, 2001). A similar diversity of inspiration and application is evident even within North America, where therapists of a constructivist and social constructionist bent have supported members of disadvantaged communities such as inner-city youth in their efforts to develop a sense of identity, voice, and initiative (Holzman & Morss, 2000; Saleebey, 1998).

In three respects at least, postmodern therapies raise ethical questions that are subtly but significantly different than those raised by traditional perspectives. First, the high respect for the client's world of meaning, combined with the relative lack of any fixed external reference point for what constitutes psychopathology, can confront the postmodern practitioner with ethical dilemmas in treating clients who do not seek therapy voluntarily and who experience their behavior and feelings as unproblematic. For example, working with eating disorders such as anorexia can be complicated in this way, as clients who organize their world around the relentless pursuit of thinness may view their "disorder" as entirely congruent with their preferred self-image (Fransella, 1993). However, some social constructionist counselors have devised creative and demonstrably effective ways of dealing with such problems, by helping clients recognize the destructive role of "dominant narratives" or oppressive cultural discourses about weight in their lives, which can be externalized and resisted (White & Epston, 1990).

The second ethical issue that characterizes postmodern work, especially that of a narrative, feminist, or culturally informed type, is the necessity to place personal problems in broader social contexts, in keeping with the overarching emphasis on cultural-linguistic features of problem construction featured in the epigenetic systems model (Mascolo et al., 1997). From this perspective it becomes ethically essential to critique and "deconstruct" oppressive discourses in the broader culture, including the "culture" of our own profession (Holzman & Morss, 2000). A radical example of this is the organization of "anti-anorexia" leagues, in which clients struggling with eating disorders join together to deface billboards glorifying anorexic models (Madigan & Goldman, 1998).

Finally, a third issue that could be construed as broadly ethical in its implications concerns the willingness of advocates of any given form of therapy to subject their preferred approach to rigorous evaluation of its effectiveness. Most contemporary constructivists, no less than advocates of cognitive-behavioral therapy, support this goal, but they differ in their preferred approach to this ethical mandate. Thus, constructivists take seriously the growing consensus that most forms of responsible psychotherapy enjoy considerable support, but very little evidence has emerged for the superiority of one school or approach over others. Although such claims continue to be propounded, a great deal of evidence now suggests that the lion's share of outcome in psychotherapy is attributable to *client* variables, such as psychological mindedness, and factors common to most or all therapies, such as the quality of the working alliance (Messer & Wampold, 2002). Indeed, quantitative reviews of controlled outcome studies report that, once investigator allegiance is taken into account, apparent differences favoring the efficacy of one approach over another vanish (Robinson, Berman, & Neimeyer, 1990), and it has been found that over 70% of the difference in efficacy observed in primary studies is accounted for by the advocacy of the researcher for one treatment over another (Luborsky et al., 2002). Underscoring this conclusion, carefully randomized comparative trials in which investigators did not favor one treatment (e.g., cognitive-behavioral therapy) over the other (e.g., mutual support groups) report no differences in the outcome of the respective treatment conditions (Bright, Baker, & Neimeyer, 1999).

In keeping with this growing evidence base, constructivist psychotherapy researchers have generally been less interested in "horse race" comparisons of their preferred approaches and competitors and more oriented toward conducting basic research on those psychological structures and change processes that are relevant to the refinement of all therapy, regardless of its pedigree. For example, researchers have focused on adducing evidence for the reliability and validity of such constructivist assessment techniques as laddering (R. A. Neimeyer et al., 2001), repertory and implications grids (Dempsey & Neimeyer, 1995; Feixas, Moliner, Montes, Mari, & Neimeyer, 1992; Fransella & Bannister, 1977), and various forms of content and narrative coding (Angus, 1992; Viney, 1988). In addition to reassuring clinicians about the psychometric adequacy of these assessment methods, such studies also lend credibility to constructivist models of meaning systems, whose structure and change across the course of therapy have been traced in literally hundreds of studies (Hardison & Neimeyer, 2007; Winter, 1992).

This penchant for process-outcome research notwithstanding, constructivists also have conducted conventional controlled trials of the efficacy of their preferred treatments, finding evidence for their general efficacy in reducing the symptomatology clients report at the outset of therapy (see Holland, Neimeyer, Currier, & Berman, 2007; Viney, Metcalfe, & Winter, 2005, for reviews), with some suggestive evidence that such treatments may be especially effective in helping clients struggling with high levels of anxiety, whereas they seem to be less useful in dealing with serious disorders of a psychotic kind (Holland & Neimeyer, in press). Significantly, however, constructivist researchers have been as active in investigating change processes in other therapeutic modalities (e.g., psychodynamic, group, behavioral) as in their own (Greenberg, Elliott, & Lietaer, 1994; Levitt & Angus, 1999). For example, although both constructivist and interpersonal process-oriented approaches to group therapy with incest survivors are demonstrably effective (Alexander, Neimeyer, & Follette, 1991; Alexander, Neimeyer, Follette, Moore, & Harter, 1989), further study of the group dynamics in each condition indicates that over a quarter of the variance in outcome reflects processes of identification first with group members and then with group therapists over time (R. A. Neimeyer, Harter, & Alexander, 1991). Such a strategy of investigating basic change processes is arguably more relevant to improving our understanding of the mechanisms of action in psychotherapy than a single-minded attempt to demonstrate the superiority of a preferred treatment.

The growing contributions of constructivism to the empirical study of psychotherapy notwithstanding, some postmodern theorists and practitioners are skeptical of the relevance of much psychotherapy research, viewing it as more concerned with advancing the power and prestige of professionals than with serving the interests of clients (Parker, 2000). Even from the standpoint of loyal scientist-practitioners working from a constructivist base, there is reason to acknowledge the "essential tension" between the necessary simplification and formalism of outcome research and the slippery subtlety of that relational renegotiation of meaning called psychotherapy (R. A. Neimeyer, 2000). Perhaps the most realistic expectation is that research can tell us something of a general sort about the "active ingredients" of therapeutic change, although the delicate dance of connection between a given client and therapist will always require an intuitive "read" of what is possible and necessary at each moment of therapeutic encounter (R. A. Neimeyer, 2002).

# 30

# Constructing an integrative practice

Given the profusion of approaches to psychotherapy—even cognitive-behavioral approaches—it is not surprising that many psychotherapy theorists, and many more practitioners, have for the last 20 years or more advocated some form of integration of the disparate models and methods (Goldfried, 1995; Norcross, 1986). Ironically, however, approaches to psychotherapy integration are themselves multiple, with each differing importantly in its assumptions and objectives (R. A. Neimeyer, 1993b). At the least ambitious end of the continuum, integration might simply mean *technical eclecticism*, tolerating or encouraging the therapist's adopting "whatever works," or seems to work, in assisting a given client (Whitaker & Keith, 1981). Though common in practice, it is rarely championed by psychotherapy scholars and researchers, because its unsystematic penchant to borrow any superficially attractive technique in the absence of orienting principles or heuristics leaves the therapist rudderless in the often uncharted waters of psychotherapeutic process—interpreting transference patterns at one moment, disputing irrational thoughts at another, and using paradoxical interventions at a third. As an alternative, in *systematic eclecticism* the therapist selects an approach—such as directive, behavioral interventions or more exploratory, emotion-focused work—depending on the characteristics of the client, such as his or her degree of "psychological reactance" to being controlled by another, or tendency to construe life problems in externalizing or internalizing terms (Beutler & Clarkin, 1990). Although the attempt to inform therapist intuition about "what to use when" with data-based predictions is commendable, evidence concerning the effectiveness of this "matching" orientation is equivocal

(Baker & Neimeyer, 2003). More fundamentally, it could be claimed that even a successful program of systematic technical eclecticism would represent not so much a form of psychotherapy *integration* as a form of systematic *pluralism*, permitting more informed switching between orientations without promoting their assimilation into a larger, more coherent, conceptual framework.

Finally, and most ambitiously, some psychotherapy scholars have advocated for true *theoretical integration*, whereby two or more different approaches to psychotherapy would be merged to form a more encompassing theory of human problems and principles of change (Wachtel, 1991). The bringing together of originally distinct behavioral and cognitive therapies into a hybrid cognitive-behavioral model reflects one such progressive integration, yielding an offspring theory that is arguably more comprehensive and technically diverse than either of its parents considered alone. However, the promise of psychotherapy integration at this conceptual level can only be realized if principles are identified that assist in the identification of candidate theories that can contribute coherently to a more overarching theoretical framework (Messer, 1987).

As a step in this direction, I have elsewhere sketched the outlines of an approach that I have termed *theoretically progressive integration* or TPI (R. A. Neimeyer, 1993b; Neimeyer & Feixas, 1990). At the heart of this perspective is a concern with *epistemological* criteria for integration, criteria concerned with the basic approaches to knowledge that shape the various theories to be integrated. In this view each system of psychotherapy embodies a distinctive set of epistemological commitments, ranging from core, often implicit, *metatheoretical beliefs* about the nature of reality and human beings' relationship to that reality, through *formal theories* of human functioning and *clinical theories* of the nature of human distress and disorder, to therapeutic *strategies and techniques*. By implication, the ideal candidate approaches for psychotherapy integration would be different models of therapy that showed strong convergence at core levels, but considerable diversity at strategic levels, offering the twin advantages of conceptual coherence and technical expansion when merged into a more comprehensive model. It is just this kind of core compatibility in metatheory that characterizes constructivist psychotherapies, which offer a great deal of variety in specific procedures. As a result, adventurous clinicians looking to add to their toolbox of techniques while remaining theoretically consistent can find in constructivism a rich trove of concepts and methods to enrich their practice. This has certainly been my experience across the years, as illustrated in the following substantial case study of constructivist psychotherapy. By sharing it in some detail I hope to convey something of the fluidity and scope of constructivist practice, in a way that is responsive to the shifting needs of clients, and the shifting competencies of therapists as well.

Bill W was a 43-year-old mid-level manager who was referred to therapy by his company's employee-assistance program (EAP) when his symptoms of anxiety proved unresponsive to the brief, cognitive-behavioral therapy he had been offered. On his first consultation with me, Bill described his life as a "roller coaster" over the last five years, culminating in his leaving his wife, Sally, after some 17 years of marriage. Importantly, the fault lines of the divorce also opened a structural chasm within the family, as the couple's 15-year-old son, Randy, remained with his father, while their 12-year-old daughter, Cassie, moved with her mother to a distant state. Bill was candid in his first session about the immediate precipitant for the divorce: his clandestine relationship with Delanie, a 39-year-old divorced employee in the same firm who "knew how to treat him," in contrast to the "forceful, argumentative, confrontational" interactions he had long had with Sally. Although the distance from his ex-wife mitigated the friction between them, a number of other problems had seemed to crowd in to take its place, including increasingly "testy" interactions with Randy, whose grades were slipping at school, a recent mediocre annual evaluation that served as a "wake up call" about his own performance on the job, and, above all, the escalating anxiety that had broken through in the form of a handful of anxiety attacks. Having no previous experience in therapy beyond the brief EAP contact, Bill was nonetheless eager to "figure out what was happening to him" with the assistance of an "objective observer," given his conviction that "talking helped." Thus began a complex therapeutic journey that spanned some 18 months of approximately bi-weekly sessions, which focused principally on the dyadic-relational and personal-agentic spheres of his life.

In subsequent sessions Bill soon elaborated on his presenting problems, noting how he was "running behind schedule" with Delanie, who was eager for a more open and public relationship and one that might eventually lead to greater commitment. Despite the "solid ground" on which Bill felt their relationship was built, he confessed to a strong reluctance to move more visibly in this direction, a reluctance that was only partly explainable in terms of the anti-nepotism rules at work that led them to keep their intimacy a secret. At the same time, Bill could feel his daughter Cassie growing "cooler and more distant" with each passing month, particularly since his anxiety had peaked in preparation for his driving to visit her, leading him to cancel the trip. Observing Bill's seeming impasse at this dyadic-relational level, I suggested that he invite Delanie to join us for the fourth session as a "consultant" to his therapy, an invitation she accepted on the condition that therapy remain focused on "his problems."

The session that followed was enlightening, as Delanie eagerly shared her impression of Bill as a "procrastinator" who was "dragging his feet" in committing to her. For her own part, Delanie described herself as a "risk taker" who was eager to "move ahead" in their relationship, and saw a greater involvement between Bill's children and herself to be the next crucial step in that direction. My efforts to allow each to articulate his or her view of both the problem and their visions of their future prompted mutual statements of caring and respect and a sense of "closeness" that Bill underscored in his opening remarks in our subsequent individual session. At the same time, however, Bill had experienced still greater distance with Cassie, precipitated by guilt over being unable to fly to visit her on her birthday because of a crippling flight phobia. Further inquiry confirmed what I had suspected: for Bill the problems of his relationship to Delanie and Cassie were intricately interwoven, as he could not imagine forcing his reluctant daughter to meet the woman who she blamed for ending her parents' marriage. As he began to voice this sentiment explicitly, Bill remarked that "a part of him would feel relieved to break up with Delanie," apparently as a way of resolving his standoff with his daughter. Although he quickly drew back from this conclusion, it was clear that the prospect of marriage was freighted with important emotional meanings that made remaining single the preferred, if denied option. I therefore sought to tease out the higher order implications of this choice using laddering technique, the results of which are summarized in Figure 4.

As the laddering revealed, the unspoken implications of remaining single for Bill included *being free*, *having fewer hassles*, *feeling productive*, and experiencing *life as good, the way things ought to be*. In contrast, marriage for him entailed the subjective meanings of being *constrained*, experiencing *conflicts*, *feeling destructive*, and regarding life as *stressful* and *uncomfortable*. Immediately after completing this hierarchy of constructs, Bill jolted upright and stated, "It just occurred to me that I'm describing my first marriage!" There then followed a probing discussion of how the sense of constriction and conflict in Bill's relationship with Sally was "bleeding over" into his relationship with Delanie, paralyzing him from "moving forward" as, at a more conscious level, he apparently wanted. As the session neared its close, Bill noted enthusiastically, "Now I *really* feel like I'm in therapy!"

Despite this important step, Bill made little progress in the coming few sessions toward committing more clearly to Delanie or promoting her greater involvement with his children. The

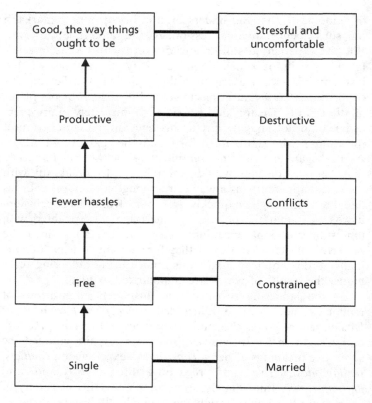

**Figure 4** Personal construct ladder for Bill W

tension—both intrapersonal and interpersonal—over this dead-lock mounted with a second impending trip to visit Cassie some 500 miles away. As Bill identified his "mysterious jitteriness" over the trip, I took this as an implicit request for help in understanding its meaning, and asked him to close his eyes and direct his attention to the bodily "felt sense" associated with the emotion. Drawing on Gendlin's (1996) focusing technique, I asked him to "stay with" the feeling and attempt to give it voice. Bill sat quiet for a moment, then noted that he felt "alone," then "lonesome," despite Delanie's having volunteered to drive the distance with him and stay supportively in the hotel room as Bill went to spend the day with his daughter. Wrinkling his brow, Bill then became aware of the inner complexity of the feeling that was emerging: the "jitteriness" also carried emotional connotations of "undermining Delanie's trust in him" as he flashed to an image of becoming too anxious to be able to drive. Further processing of this self-awareness led Bill to identify and articulate his sense of not only losing self-control but also letting down those he loved, including "disappointing God." The subsequent joint session with Delanie corroborated this relational tension, as Bill tearfully acknowledged "feeling stuck in the middle" in relation to Delanie and Cassie, risking losing one if he moved closer to the other. The tragic dynamic was underscored by Delanie, who emphasized that, "Only a part of this is about Cassie—the rest is about Bill," adding through her own tears that she "deserved better than to spend the rest of her life alone." Under Delanie's ultimatum that they make the trip together and that Bill arrange at least fleeting contact between her and Cassie, Bill capitulated. However, this plan, though technically successful, precipitated deep fears of marginalization on Delanie's part, expressed in the form of such uncontrolled sobbing on the drive home that she experienced trouble breathing. Thus, it was little surprise that she began distancing self-protectively in the ensuing week.

At this unfortunate juncture I found myself verging on departure for a month-long speaking trip to Australia and New Zealand, with only a single session with Bill left before my leave taking. I therefore sensed that we were at a choice point—should we delve deeply into the source of Bill's torment at the risk of leaving him vulnerable and unsupported during my absence or focus on reinforcing Bill's means of coping with his distressing situation until I could return? Prompted by Bill's apparent readiness (and need) to "understand what was happening to him," I opted for the former. Perhaps influenced by my pending visit to narrative therapy colleagues, I therefore began a sustained externalizing conversation with Bill about the "guilt" that he blamed for "making it impossible for him to look at Randy and Cassie and tell them he was going to marry Delanie." The result was a powerful review, prompted by my "curious questioning" about the influence of guilt in Bill's life, but given direction by his detailed and evocative replies. Following the hour, I drafted and mailed Bill a letter that captured the essence of our session, drawing heavily upon his own expressions of his situation, and integrating the insights that had emerged for him in the course of our conversation. The letter, in its entirety, read:

Dear Bill

After our session today I found myself thinking more about your bold recognition that guilt is at the core of your difficulties, and needed to be dealt with directly if you are going to get your life back on track. As you said, "I can't continue with my life the way I have been going with my life. Until I take care of myself, I can't deal with anyone else." You went on to note quite a few ways that guilt was having a negative impact on your life:

1  It requires you to be uncomfortable in all of your close relationships.
2  It prevents you from enjoying yourself with abandon with Delanie.
3  It forces you to "distance" yourself from Delanie, and remain uncommitted about the future of your relationship.
4  It keeps you from "taking a position" with your kids.
5  It forces you to conceal the history of your relationship with Delanie, and to keep secrets from those you love.

6   It condemns you to doing unending penance for the "sin" you have committed.

I was very moved by your declaration that "I'm reaching a point that I can't take it anymore; I'm tired of everybody beating on me, and I've got to do something about it." I'm sure you are right about this and that you are indeed correct in directly confronting the destructive influence of guilt on your life. Discussing with your minister the nature of your "sin," as you suggested, and the actions necessary for forgiveness seems to be a bold and creative step in this direction. I was also struck by your idea of talking quite forthrightly with the kids about your history with Delanie, although it might be wise not to move too quickly in eliminating guilt in this way, given the important role that it has played in your life up until this time.

As I leave to spend some time in Australia and New Zealand, I will take with me a good deal of curiosity about these intriguing developments in your life, and I look forward to an update when we get back together. Good luck.

> Yours,
> Bob Neimeyer

The following session, held just over one month later upon my return, was something of a turning point. Bill opened with the remark that the letter I had sent him was "great," because "it recapped our last meeting better than he ever could." He then recounted an impressive series of "unique outcomes," instances in which he was "winning his life back from guilt" through undertaking small carpentry projects, going camping, and doing other things he had long neglected because they seemed "selfish." At the same time, he announced that he felt "some of the fire coming back" to see Delanie, who continued to interpose some distance between them. Interestingly, he also had spontaneously showed the letter to Delanie, who responded by taking it to discuss with her own counselor, because she suspected it had actually been written as an indirect therapeutic communication to describe *her*! As a result, she had asked Bill's permission to join him for the next session, so that she could uncover the role of guilt in her own life and her relationship to Bill and his children.

The next session was relationally clarifying, but initially stalemated: Bill increasingly resented Delanie's demands to be more involved with his children, which echoed for him some of the worst aspects of his previous marriage. Likewise, Delanie increasingly questioned Bill's commitment to her because of his unwillingness to "bring together his two separate lives." As a result, each intensified his or her behavior in a way that was coherent with his or her construction of the situation, but that also validated the partner's interpretation. This pernicious validational cycle is depicted in the bow-tie diagram in Figure 5. Mapping this "dance of despair" for them, I was gratified by Bill's response that it was "a recipe for a holding pattern if ever there was one. The stability makes sense, because the pattern gets reinforced over time." Delanie concurred, and added that it felt good to know that "it's not just that one of us is flawed or crazy."

The next several sessions continued this progress, though with occasional setbacks. For example, Bill reported "feeling more and more like his old self, more relaxed and focused," to the point of taking Delanie on a public date, their first in their two-year relationship. Furthermore, he even courageously had a heart-to-heart talk with his preacher about his affair and divorce, characterizing the minister as "tacitly forgiving." The one domain in which little headway was made was in involving Delanie with Cassie, as he planned a solo visit to see his daughter. As a father–daughter visit, the trip was remarkable for Bill's degree of risk taking; he even read her a carefully prepared letter in his hotel room reaffirming his love for her and asking her to forgive him for the divorce "when she was ready." A subsequent, non-accusatory letter followed to his ex-wife,

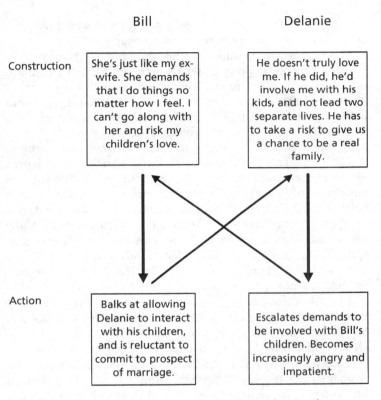

**Figure 5** "Bow tie" linking levels of construction and action for Bill and Delanie

Sally, explaining the reasons for their estrangement in terms of their "basically different views of life." Gradually, Delanie softened, moving slowly from feeling "totally excluded, almost invisible" in the realignment of Bill's family, to a more empathetic stance. Couple sessions were often marked by poignant emotion but also deepened connection. As Bill formulated it through a haze of tears in one session, "Delanie's willingness to compromise and understand is exactly what made me fall in love with her." As Delanie moved close to him and wiped her own eyes, he added, "She gives me power through her love."

The remaining months of this episode of therapy were characterized by growing closeness between Bill and Delanie— both agreed that the relationship was "stronger than ever"— although the rare visits to or from Cassie remained fraught with anxiety. This was compounded by an intensification of Bill's longstanding flight phobia, which he described as a "fear of being closed in, unable to get out." Not only was his inability to travel by air complicating his executive work life, but it was also, and even more seriously, slowing his reconnection with his daughter. Bill therefore eagerly accepted my referral to a behavioral colleague who offered an *in vivo* desensitization program for flight phobia in the hope of freeing himself of the constraints it imposed in both the personal and professional spheres. Our planned contact ended on this relatively optimistic note, with Bill noting in his closing session, "It is silly to lose my relationship with Delanie over my reluctance to commit."

I heard nothing more from Bill over the ensuing four years, until he called to request another session. In many respects, Bill had consolidated his therapeutic gains over this interval: he and Delanie had been happily married for nearly three years, he credited his stronger parenting with Randy with helping his son straighten out his school problems and get through a difficult breakup with his girlfriend, and he and Delanie had worked out their respective careers in a way that supported their continued professional development. But two problems stubbornly persisted: the flight phobia, as he did not feel sufficient "trust" in the behavior therapist to continue beyond four sessions, and the "tug of war" between Cassie and Delanie, which had contributed to his having no contact with his daughter except through correspondence for three years. Indeed, despite the civility of their earlier contacts, Cassie's letters had been unequivocal in stating that she "could never accept Delanie and did not want to see her." Thus, Bill was left in a deep quandary, and was seeking my help "to stand up, be a man, and do what's right."

Of course, Bill was not the only one of us to experience personal and professional growth during the hiatus in our relationship. I too had developed as a postmodern therapist, incorporating new concepts and methods—such as those associated with coherence therapy—that were themselves coherent with my earlier ways of working while moving them in a more consistently experiential direction. In a sense, our earlier sessions had tacked back and forth between Bill's initially external, factual narratives and my frequently reflexive, meaning-oriented interventions, helping him shift from the brute "facts" of his problem to their personal significance. Now, however, I was more inclined to promote a sustained internal, emotional exploration of a problematic position in order to help clients encounter and articulate the powerful but unstated premises that sustained their symptomatic behavior. Viewing Bill's chronic complaint from this coherence perspective, I now more clearly construed his motivation to transcend the pattern of anxious avoidance of Cassie as an *anti-symptom position* that motivated his return to therapy. The pain this "stand off" caused him was very real, and my first tasks in the session were to help him articulate it and to respond to it with genuine empathy. But my ultimate task was to help him encounter the problem's higher order, hidden purpose, that system of meanings and intentions that constituted his unconscious *pro-symptom position*. Much of the session therefore consisted of *radical inquiry*, the goal of which was to lead Bill to "bump into" these deeply embedded constructs in an experientially vivid way, without in any way attempting to interpret, invalidate or challenge them. Once both the anti-symptom and pro-symptom stances were in clear view, I hoped his painfully repetitive story of his relationship with his daughter would make a new kind of sense, setting the stage for the conscious affirmation of one position or the other or the possible integration of both into a more comprehensive self narrative.

Using the technique of *symptom deprivation*, I began by asking Bill to close his eyes and "get a clear visual picture of

Delanie and Cassie together, engaged in some ordinary, day-to-day activity," to prompt his awareness of how he would experience "reality" deprived of the customary distance he maintained between them. After a moment of silence, Bill visibly winced, and said, "I wanted to say it would be wonderful, but my first reaction was to break out into a cold sweat. I immediately flashed to a big confrontation between two stubborn people." Intrigued, I instructed him to simply sit with this scene for a few more moments and to "let me know if anything else came up." This triggered the *serial accessing* of felt meanings, in which he first noted with a trembling jaw that the emotion that washed over him "felt exactly like the internal panic over getting on board a plane." He then swallowed hard, opened his eyes, and said, "It may not even be Delanie and Cassie together—it may be *me* and Cassie together that's the problem." He fell silent for a moment more, then added, "I've got something I can't break through here."

Rather than shifting to an abstract discussion of this impasse, I used the technique of *sentence completion* to keep Bill in contact with the further implications of this pro-symptom position. This involved my inviting him, without pre-reflection, to complete the stem, "If Cassie were to come here, then . . . ." His first response was predictable and safe: " . . . we'd be happy to see her." His second went deeper: " . . . I'd be nervous about losing one or both of them." As his eyes moistened, I prompted him with a third, more personal stem, to which he replied, "If Cassie were to come here, then *I* . . . might see her walk out of my life." Wiping away tears, Bill then flashed to an image of Cassie at age nine, as he sat snuggled up with her, telling her she'd soon be a teenager and "all grown up." Putting her arms around his neck, she had lovingly reassured him, "I'll always be your little girl." Tears welled in Bill's eyes, and he removed his glasses to wipe them away, sobbing silently.

With all of the elements of his pro-symptom position now in view, Bill's deeper purpose in maintaining the distance with Cassie became clear, despite its great costs in their relationship as well as his new marriage. Bringing the session to a close, I formulated this stance in sharply etched words on an index card, which I handed to Bill and asked him to read slowly aloud: "As painful as this present stand off is, I would rather suffer this terrible distance from Cassie than to have her walk away and never feel her arms around my neck, never hear her say, 'I'm still your little girl'." Choking on the word "arms," Bill stammered out the sentence, and drying his tears, quietly noted that inhabiting this position consciously "made me understand the things I've been doing in a whole different light." My request that he simply read the card a few times a day, with no attempt to change his behavior, cultivated a deeper appreciation of his intentions, whose fruits became evident in our final follow-up session scheduled for one month later.

Bill returned for our final session looking somehow younger and stronger, with the deep lines of worry I had grown accustomed to seeing now less visibly etched on his brow. Behavioral progress was, if anything, even more visible: he had sent direct, but compassionate letters to Sally, urging her to "bury the hatchet" for the sake of the children; to Randy, expressing his need for the young man to "respect" Delanie, for the sake of their "special father–son relationship"; and to Delanie, offering comfort and perspective on various concerns and feelings she had had since the death of her beloved father some two years before. Most remarkably, he had also drafted a letter to Cassie, raising the topic of another visit, promising to continue the weekly phone calls he had initiated since our last session and noting that future letters would be sent from him and Delanie together. Significantly, Bill noted that he was "doing this because he could no longer live with the stand off, not because of pressure from Delanie." These clear shifts suggested that the pro-symptom position brought to light in the previous session had now begun to be dissolved in the light of Bill's awareness, opening as real behavioral options actions that were previously "off limits" at an unconscious level.

A follow-up phone call from Bill three months later confirmed this progress, and provided evidence of a further surprising development: Bill had actually taken an airplane—his first in over a decade—for his work and had scheduled a flight to visit Cassie as well. Somehow, he said, he no longer felt the fear of "enclosure" as intensely, though he couldn't say why. Bill's therapy therefore illustrates both the explicit and unspecifiable processes of therapeutic change, as well as the use of a number of postmodern procedures to map a client's meaning system, clarify his relational patterns, instigate deepened reflexivity, and consolidate the emerging contours of a preferred life narrative. It also underscores the extent to which therapists no less than clients grow as persons and professionals, a growth that is supported and prompted by the continuously evolving practice of postmodern psychotherapy.

# Conclusion

As a philosophically sophisticated, practically useful, and empirically responsive orientation to clinical practice, constructivism seems likely to continue to prosper in the decades to come. However, factors both internal to postmodern approaches and external to them are likely to affect the speed and direction of such growth, fostering the extension of these perspectives in some areas, while inhibiting them in others.

Facilitative factors that are likely to promote the further extension of constructivist, social constructionist, and narrative approaches include their remarkable flexibility in conceptualizing constraints on people's lives that originate at many levels, ranging from the individual through cultural, and their creative generation of a broad and expanding array of techniques for assessing and enlarging systems of meaning. These same factors make these approaches congenial to both humanistic psychologists who cherish client uniqueness, and radical-critical therapists who strive to deconstruct the role of oppressive cultural discourses that subjugate individuals and groups. External factors, such as the increasing ethnic, cultural, and lifestyle diversity of many nations, also encourage the development of perspectives that make fewer assumptions about what constitutes "normal" or "abnormal" behavior but that instead offer a subtle range of concepts and methods for respectfully engaging the diversity of human experience. The push for briefer therapies further bodes well for postmodern approaches to working with individuals, families, and groups that share an optimistic emphasis on human change processes and their facilitation through efficient experiential procedures. Finally, the current trend toward integration of diverse psychotherapies is congenial to a multifaceted postmodern perspective, which has influenced contemporary developments in traditions ranging from the psychodynamic through the humanistic to cognitive, and in contexts embracing individuals, families, and groups. However, the strong epistemological orientation of constructivist and social constructionist theorists also leads them to caution against an indiscriminate gallimaufry of principles and procedures, and instead to advocate only selective integration of perspectives that share key metatheoretical commitments (Messer, 1987; R. A. Neimeyer, 1993b).

On the other hand, the same richness and subtlety that make postmodern ideas attractive to seasoned clinicians of several schools probably also impedes their acceptance by developing student clinicians, who often prefer the apparent simplicity of more rule-governed, prescriptive approaches. Likewise, the commitment to the delicate interplay of client and therapist meanings in the process of therapy that characterizes constructivist and social constructionist work poses challenges to psychotherapy researchers who prefer to test the average benefit of standardized interventions to a defined diagnostic category of clients. Although those constructivist approaches whose efficacy has been assessed have fared favorably (Greenberg et al., 1994; Holland et al., 2007), the tendency of constructivist researchers to group patients by issues (e.g., "unfinished business") rather than psychiatric diagnosis (e.g., generalized anxiety disorder) militates against their inclusion in approved lists of "evidence-based practices" for particular disorders, no matter how many such controlled studies are conducted. More seriously, perhaps, the revolutionary spirit of "resistance" against aspects of mainstream approaches that postmodernists consider oppressive and pathologizing can prove threatening to powerful interests in the discipline of clinical psychology, which tend to gravitate toward more conservative, replicable forms of therapy that seem to offer the twin advantages of mass dissemination and differentiation from the "products" offered by other competing therapeutic professions.

In summary, constructivist approaches to clinical practice, like all models of psychotherapy, offer a unique and evolving distillation of intellectual and cultural trends, which are turned toward the practical goal of improving the human condition. I hope that the concepts, procedures, and case illustrations I have described in this book offer something of value to you as you continue your own efforts to engage the problems and prospects in the lives of the individuals, families, and communities with whom you work.

# References

Adams-Webber, J. R. (2001) "Prototypicality of self and evaluating others in terms of 'fuzzy' constructs", *Journal of Constructivist Psychology*, 14: 315–324.

Alexander, P. C., Neimeyer, R. A. and Follette, V. M. (1991) "Group therapy for women sexually abused as children: A controlled study and investigation of individual differences", *Journal of Interpersonal Violence*, 6: 219–231.

Alexander, P. C., Neimeyer, R. A., Follette, V. M., Moore, M. K. and Harter, S. L. (1989) "A comparison of group treatments of women sexually abused as children", *Journal of Consulting and Clinical Psychology*, 57: 479–483.

Allport, G. W. (1961) *Pattern and Growth in Personality*. New York: Holt.

Angus, L. E. (1992) "Metaphor and the communication interaction in psychotherapy", in S. G. Toukmanian and D. L. Rennie (eds), *Psychotherapy Process Research*, pp. 187–210. Newbury Park, CA: Sage.

Appignanesi, R. and Garratt, C. (1995) *Postmodernism for Beginners*. Cambridge, UK: Icon/Penguin.

Arciero, G. and Guidano, V. (2000) "Experience, explanation, and the quest for coherence", in R. A. Neimeyer and J. D. Raskin (eds), *Constructions of Disorder*, pp. 91–117. Washington, DC: American Psychological Association.

Baker, K. D. and Neimeyer, R. A. (2003) "Therapist training and client characteristics as predictors of treatment response to group therapy for depression", *Psychotherapy Research*, 13: 135–151.

Bateson, G. (1972) *Steps to an Ecology of Mind*. New York: Dutton.

Beck, A. T. (1993) "Cognitive therapy: Past, present, and future", *Journal of Consulting and Clinical Psychology*, 61: 194–198.

Beutler, L. E. and Clarkin, J. F. (1990) *Systematic Treatment Selection*. New York: Brunner Mazel.

Bohart, A. C. and Tallman, K. (1999) *How Clients Make Therapy Work*. Washington, DC: American Psychological Association.

Bright, J. I., Baker, K. D. and Neimeyer, R. A. (1999) "Professional and paraprofessional group treatments for depression: A comparison of cognitive-behavioral and mutual support interventions", *Journal of Consulting and Clinical Psychology*, 67: 491–501.

Brown, L. S. (2000a) "Discomforts of the powerless", in R. A. Neimeyer and J. D. Raskin (eds), *Constructions of Disorder*, pp. 287–308. Washington, DC: American Psychological Association.

Brown, L. S. (2000b) "Feminist therapy", in C. R. Snyder and R. E. Ingram (eds), *Handbook of Psychological Change*, pp. 358–380. New York: Wiley.

Buber, M. (1970) *I and thou*. New York: Charles Scribner's Sons.

Dempsey, D. J. and Neimeyer, R. A. (1995) "Organization of personal knowledge: Convergent validity of implications grids and repertory grids as measures of system structure", *Journal of Constructivist Psychology*, 8: 251–261.

Derrida, J. (1978) *Writing and Difference*. Chicago: University of Chicago Press.

DiLollo, A., Neimeyer, R. A. and Manning, W. H. (2002) "A personal construct psychology view of relapse: Indications for a narrative therapy component to stuttering treatment", *Journal of Fluency Disorders*, 27: 19–42.

Ecker, B. and Hulley, L. (1996) *Depth-oriented Brief Therapy*. San Francisco: Jossey-Bass.

Ecker, B. and Hulley, L. (2000) "The order in clinical 'disorder': Symptom coherence in depth-oriented brief therapy", in R. A. Neimeyer and J. D. Raskin (eds), *Constructions of Disorder*, pp. 63–90. Washington, DC: American Psychological Association.

Ecker, B. and Hulley, L. (2008) "Coherence therapy: Swift change at the roots of symptom production", in J. D. Raskin and S. K. Bridges (eds), *Studies in Meaning*, Vol. 3, pp. 57–84. New York: Pace University Press.

Ecker, B. and Toomey, B. (2008) "Depotentiation of symptom-producing implicit memory in coherence therapy", *Journal of Constructivist Psychology*, 21: 87–150.

Efran, J. S. and Cook, P. F. (2000) "Linguistic ambiguity as a diagnostic tool", in R. A. Neimeyer and J. D. Raskin (eds), *Constructions of Disorder*, pp. 121–143. Washington, DC: American Psychological Association.

Efran, J. S. and Fauber, R. L. (1995) "Radical constructivism: Questions and answers", in R. A. Neimeyer and M. J. Mahoney (eds), *Constructivism in Psychotherapy*, pp. 275–302. Washington, DC: American Psychological Association.

Efran, J. S., Lukens, M. D. and Lukens, R. J. (1990) *Language, Structure, and Change*. New York: Norton.

Epston, D. and White, M. (1995) "Termination as a rite of passage: Questioning strategies for a therapy of inclusion", in R. A. Neimeyer and M. J. Mahoney (eds), *Constructivism in Psychotherapy*, pp. 339–356. Washington, DC: American Psychological Association.

Eron, J. B. and Lund, T. W. (1996) *Narrative Solutions in Brief Therapy*. New York: Guilford Press.

Feixas, G. (1992) "Personal construct approaches to family therapy", in R. A. Neimeyer and G. J. Neimeyer (eds), *Advances in Personal Construct Psychology*, Vol. 2, pp. 217–255. Greenwich, CT: JAI Press.

Feixas, G. (1995) "Personal constructs in systemic practice", in R. A. Neimeyer and M. J. Mahoney (eds), *Constructivism in Psychotherapy*, pp. 305–337. Washington, DC: American Psychological Association.

Feixas, G., Geldschlager, H. and Neimeyer, R. A. (2002) "Content analysis of personal constructs", *Journal of Personal Construct Psychology*, 15: 1–19.

Feixas, G., Moliner, J. L., Montes, J. N., Mari, M. T. and Neimeyer, R. A. (1992) "The stability of structural measures derived from repertory grids", *International Journal of Personal Construct Psychology*, 5(1), 25–40.

Fireman, G. D., McVay, T. E. and Flanagan, O. J. (eds) (2003) *Narrative and Consciousness*. New York: Oxford University Press.

Foucault, M. (1970) *The Order of Things*. New York: Pantheon.

Frankel, Z. F. and Levitt, H. M. (2006) "Postmodern strategies for working with resistance: Problem resolution or self-revolution?" *Journal of Constructivist Psychology*, 19: 219–250.

Frankel, Z. F., Levitt, H. M., Murray, D. M., Greenberg, L. S. and Angus, L. E. (2006) "Assessing psychotherapy silences: An empirically derived categorization system and sampling strategy", *Psychotherapy Research*, 16: 627–638.

Fransella, F. (1993) "The construct of resistance in psychotherapy", in

L. Leitner and G. Dunnett (eds), *Critical Issues in Personal Construct Psychology*, pp. 117–134. Malabar, CA: Krieger.

Fransella, F. and Bannister, D. (1977) *A Manual for Repertory Grid Technique*. New York: Academic Press.

Fransella, F., Bell, R. and Bannister, D. (2004) *A Manual for Repertory Grid Technique*, 2nd edn. Chichester, UK: Wiley.

Freeman, J., Epston, D. and Lobovits, D. (1997) *Playful Approaches to Serious Problems*. New York: Norton.

Freud, S. (1964) "An outline of psycho-analysis", in *Standard Edition*, Vol. 23. London: Hogarth Press. (Originally published 1940)

Gendlin, E. T. (1996) *Focusing-oriented Psychotherapy*. New York: Guilford Press.

Gergen, K. J. (1991) *The Saturated Self*. New York: Basic Books.

Gergen, K. J. (1999) *An Invitation to Social Construction*. Cambridge, MA: Harvard University Press.

Goldfried, M. R. (1995) *From Cognitive-behavior Therapy to Psychotherapy Integration*. New York: Springer.

Gonçalves, M. M., Matos, M. and Santos, A. (in press) "Narrative therapy and the nature of 'innovative moments' in the construction of change", in J. D. Raskin, S. K. Bridges and R. A. Neimeyer (eds), *Studies in Meaning*, Vol. 4. New York: Pace University Press.

Greenberg, L., Elliott, R. and Lietaer, G. (1994) "Research on experiential therapies", in A. Bergin and S. Garfield (eds), *Handbook of Psychotherapy and Behavior Change*, 4th edn, pp. 509–539. New York: Wiley.

Greenberg, L., Elliott, R. and Rice, L. (1993) *Facilitating Emotional Change*. New York: Guilford Press.

Greenberg, L. S., Watson, J. C. and Lietaer, G. (eds) (1998) *Handbook of Experiential Psychotherapy*. New York: Guilford Press.

Guidano, V. F. (1991) *The Self in Process*. New York: Guilford Press.

Guidano, V. F. (1995) "Constructivist psychotherapy: A theoretical framework", in R. A. Neimeyer and M. J. Mahoney (eds), *Constructivism in Psychotherapy*, pp. 93–108. Washington, DC: American Psychological Association.

Hardison, H. and Neimeyer, R. A. (2007) "Numbers and narratives: Quantitative and qualitative convergence in constructivist assessment", *Journal of Constructivist Psychology*, 20: 285–308.

Harré, R. and Gillett, R. (1994) *The Discursive Mind*. Thousand Oaks, CA: Sage.

Harter, S. L. (1995) "Construing on the edge", in R. A. Neimeyer and M. J. Mahoney (eds), *Constructivism in Psychotherapy*, pp. 371–383. Washington, DC: American Psychological Association.

Held, B. S. (1995) *Back to Reality*. New York: Norton.

Hermans, H. (1995) *Self-narratives: The Construction of Meaning in Psychotherapy*. New York: Guilford Press.

Hermans, H. (2002) "The person as a motivated storyteller", in R. A. Neimeyer and G. J. Neimeyer (eds), *Advances in Personal Construct Psychology*, Vol. 5, pp. 3–38. Westport, CT: Praeger.

Hermans, H. and Dimaggio, G. (eds) (2004) *The Dialogical Self in Psychotherapy*. New York: Routledge.

Hinkle, D. (1965) *The Change of Personal Constructs from the Viewpoint of a Theory of Implications*. Unpublished Dissertation, The Ohio State University, Columbus, OH.

Hoffman, L. (1992) "A reflexive stance for family therapy", in S. McNamee and K. J. Gergen (eds), *Therapy as Social Construction*, pp. 7–24. Newbury Park, CA: Sage.

Holland, J. M. and Neimeyer, R. A. (in press) "The efficacy of personal construct therapy as a function of the type and severity of the presenting problem", *Journal of Constructivist Psychology*.

Holland, J., Neimeyer, R. A., Currier, J. and Berman, J. S. (2007) "The efficacy of personal construct therapy: A comprehensive review", *Journal of Clinical Psychology*, 63: 93–107.

Holzman, L. and Morss, J. (eds) (2000) *Postmodern Psychologies, Societal Practice, and Political Life*. New York: Routledge.

Jankowicz, D. (2003) *The Easy Guide to Repertory Grids*. Chichester, UK: Wiley.

Jung, C. G. (1971) "The structure of the psyche", in *The Portable Jung*, pp. 23–46. New York: Viking.

Kazantzis, N. and L'Abate, L. (eds) (2006) *Handbook of Homework Assignments in Psychotherapy*. New York: Kluwer.

Kelly, G. A. (1969) "The language of hypothesis", in B. Mahrer (ed.), *Clinical Psychology and Personality*, pp. 147–162. New York: Wiley.

Kelly, G. A. (1977) "The psychology of the unknown", in D. Bannister (ed.), *New Perspectives in Personal Construct Theory*, pp. 1–19. San Diego, CA: Academic Press.

Kelly, G. A. (1991) *The Psychology of Personal Constructs*. New York: Routledge. (Originally published 1955)

Kernberg, O. F. (1976) *Object Relations Theory and Psychoanalysis*. Northvale, NJ: Jason Aronson.

Kohut, H. (1971) *The Analysis of the Self*. New York: International Universities Press.

Lather, P. (1992) "Postmodernism and the human sciences", in S. Kvale (ed.), *Psychology and Postmodernism*, pp. 88–109. Newbury Park, CA: Sage.

Leitner, L. M. (1995) "Optimal therapeutic distance", in R. A.

Neimeyer and M. J. Mahoney (eds), *Constructivism in Psychotherapy*, pp. 357–370. Washington, DC: American Psychological Association.

Leitner, L. M. and Faidley, A. J. (1995) "The awful, aweful nature of ROLE relationships", in R. A. Neimeyer and G. J. Neimeyer (eds), *Advances in Personal Construct Psychology*, Vol. 3, pp. 291–314. Greenwich, CT: JAI Press.

Leitner, L. M. and Faidley, A. J. (2002) "Disorder, diagnosis, and the struggles of humanness", in J. D. Raskin and S. K. Bridges (eds), *Studies in Meaning*, pp. 99–121. New York: Pace University Press.

Leitner, L. M., Faidley, A. and Celantana, M. (2000) "Diagnosing human meaning making", in R. A. Neimeyer and J. D. Raskin (eds), *Constructions of Disorder*, pp. 175–203. Washington, DC: American Psychological Association.

Levitt, H. and Angus, L. (1999) "Psychotherapy process measure research and the evaluation of psychotherapy orientation", *Journal of Psychotherapy Integration*, 9: 279–300.

Levitt, H. M., Neimeyer, R. A. and Williams, D. C. (2005) "Rules versus principles in psychotherapy: Implications of the quest for universal guidelines in the movement for empirically supported treatments", *Journal of Contemporary Psychotherapy*, 35: 117–129.

Luborsky, L., Rosenthal, R., Diguer, L., Andrusyna, T. P., Berman, J. S., Levitt, J. T., et al. (2002) "The Dodo bird verdict is alive and well—Mostly", *Clinical Psychology: Science and Practice*, 9: 2–12.

Madigan, S. P. and Goldman, E. M. (1998) "A narrative approach to anorexia", in M. F. Hoyt (ed.), *Handbook of Constructive Therapies*, pp. 380–700. San Francisco: Jossey-Bass.

Mahoney, M. J. (1988) "Constructive metatheory I: Basic features and historical foundations", *International Journal of Personal Construct Psychology*, 1: 299–315.

Mahoney, M. J. (1991) *Human Change Processes*. New York: Basic Books.

Mahoney, M. J. (1993) "Theoretical developments in the cognitive psychotherapies", *Journal of Consulting and Clinical Psychology*, 61: 187–193.

Martin, J. (1994) *The Construction and Understanding of Psychotherapeutic Change*. New York: Teachers College Press.

Mascolo, M. F., Craig-Bray, L. and Neimeyer, R. A. (1997) "The construction of meaning and action in development and psychotherapy: An epigenetic systems approach", in G. J. Neimeyer and R. A. Neimeyer (eds), *Advances in Personal Construct Psychology*, Vol. 4, pp. 3–38. Greenwich, CT: JAI Press.

Messer, S. B. (1987) "Can the Tower of Babel be completed? A critique of the common language proposal", *Journal of Integrative and Eclectic Psychotherapy*, 6: 195–199.

Messer, S. B. and Wampold, B. E. (2002) "Let's face facts: Common factors are more important than specific therapy ingredients", *Clinical Psychology: Science and Practice*, 9: 21–25.

Monk, G., Winslade, J., Crocket, K. and Epston, D. (1996) *Narrative Therapy in Practice*. San Francisco: Jossey-Bass.

Neimeyer, G. J. (1992) "Personal constructs and vocational structure: A critique of poor reason", in R. A. Neimeyer and G. J. Neimeyer (eds), *Advances in Personal Construct Psychology*, Vol. 2, pp. 91–120. Greenwich, CT: JAI.

Neimeyer, G. J. (1993) *Constructivist Assessment: A Casebook*. Newbury Park, CA: Sage.

Neimeyer, G. J. and Fukuyama, M. (1984) "Exploring the content and structure of cross-cultural attitudes", *Counselor Education and Supervision*, 23: 214–224.

Neimeyer, G. J., Lee, J., Aksoy-Toska, G. and Phillip, D. (2008) "Epistemological commitments among seasoned therapists: Some practical implications of being constructivist", in J. D. Raskin and S. K. Bridges (eds), *Studies in Meaning*, Vol. 3, pp. 31–54. New York: Pace University Press.

Neimeyer, R. A. (1988) "Clinical guidelines for conducting interpersonal transaction groups", *International Journal of Personal Construct Psychology*, 1: 181–190.

Neimeyer, R. A. (1993a) "Constructivism and the cognitive therapies: Some conceptual and strategic contrasts", *Journal of Cognitive Psychotherapy*, 7: 159–171.

Neimeyer, R. A. (1993b) "Constructivism and the problem of psychotherapy integration", *Journal of Psychotherapy Integration*, 3: 133–157.

Neimeyer, R. A. (1993c) "Constructivist approaches to the measurement of meaning", in G. J. Neimeyer (ed.), *Constructivist Assessment: A Casebook*, pp. 58–103. Newbury Park: CA: Sage.

Neimeyer, R. A. (1995a) "An invitation to constructivist psychotherapies", in R. A. Neimeyer and M. J. Mahoney (eds), *Constructivism in Psychotherapy*, pp. 1–8. Washington, DC: American Psychological Association.

Neimeyer, R. A. (1995b) "Constructivist psychotherapies: Features, foundations, and future directions", in R. A. Neimeyer and M. J. Mahoney (eds), *Constructivism in Psychotherapy*, pp. 11–38. Washington, DC: American Psychological Association.

Neimeyer, R. A. (1998) "Social constructionism in the counselling context", *Counselling Psychology Quarterly*, 11: 135–149.

Neimeyer, R. A. (1999) "George Kelly", in *Encyclopedia of Psychology*. Washington, DC: American Psychological Association.

Neimeyer, R. A. (2000) "Research and practice as essential tensions: A constructivist confession", in L. M. Vaillant and S. Soldz (eds), *Empirical Knowledge and Clinical Experience*, pp. 123–150. Washington, DC: American Psychological Association.

Neimeyer, R. A. (2002) "The relational co-construction of selves: A postmodern perspective", *Journal of Contemporary Psychotherapy*, 32: 51–59.

Neimeyer, R. A. (2004) *Constructivist Psychotherapy* [video]. Washington, DC: American Psychological Association.

Neimeyer, R. A. (2006a) "Narrating the dialogical self: Toward an expanded toolbox for the counselling psychologist", *Counselling Psychology Quarterly*, 19: 105–120.

Neimeyer, R. A. (2006b) *Rainbow in the Stone*. Memphis, TN: Mercury.

Neimeyer, R. A., Anderson, A. and Stockton, L. (2001) "Snakes versus ladders: A validation of laddering technique as a measure of hierarchical structure", *Journal of Constructivist Psychology*, 14: 85–105.

Neimeyer, R. A. and Bridges, S. K. (2003) "Postmodern approaches to psychotherapy", in A. Gurman and S. Messer (eds), *Essential Psychotherapies*, 2nd edn, pp. 272–316. New York: Guilford Press.

Neimeyer, R. A. and Feixas, G. (1990) "Constructivist contributions to psychotherapy integration", *Journal of Integrative and Eclectic Psychotherapy*, 9: 4–20.

Neimeyer, R. A., Harter, S. and Alexander, P. C. (1991) "Group perceptions as predictors of outcome in the treatment of incest survivors", *Psychotherapy Research*, 1: 149–158.

Neimeyer, R. A., Klein, M. H., Gurman, A. S. and Greist, J. H. (1983) "Cognitive structure and depressive symptomatology", *British Journal of Cognitive Psychotherapy*, 1: 65–73.

Neimeyer, R. A. and Mahoney, M. J. (eds) (1995) *Constructivism in Psychotherapy*. Washington, DC: American Psychological Association.

Neimeyer, R. A. and Winter, D. A. (2006) "Personal construct therapy", in N. Kazantzis and L. L'Abate (eds), *Handbook of Homework Assignments in Psychotherapy*. New York: Kluwer.

Neisser, U. and Fivush, R. (eds) (1994) *The Remembering Self*. Cambridge, UK: Cambridge University Press.

Norcross, J. C. (1986) "Eclectic psychotherapy: An introduction and overview", in J. C. Norcross (ed.), *Handbook of Eclectic Psychotherapy*, pp. 3–24. New York: Brunner Mazel.

Palmer, P. J. (2000) *Let Your Life Speak: Listening to the Voice of Vocation*. San Francisco: Jossey-Bass.

Parker, I. (2000) "Four story-theories about and against postmodernism in psychology", in L. Holzman and J. Morss (eds), *Postmodern Psychologies*, pp. 29–47. New York: Routledge.

Polanyi, M. (1958) *Personal Knowledge*. New York: Harper.

Procter, H. G. (1987) "Change in the family construct system", in R. A. Neimeyer and G. J. Neimeyer (eds), *Personal Construct Therapy Casebook*, pp. 153–171. New York: Springer.

Raskin, J. D. and Lewandowski, A. M. (2000) "The construction of disorder as human enterprise", in R. A. Neimeyer and J. D. Raskin (eds), *Constructions of Disorder*, pp. 15–39. Washington, DC: American Psychological Association.

Rennie, D. L. (1992) "Qualitative analysis of the client's experience of psychotherapy", in S. G. Toukmanian and D. L. Rennie (eds), *Psychotherapy Process Research*, pp. 211–233. Newbury Park, CA: Sage.

Robinson, L. A., Berman, J. S. and Neimeyer, R. A. (1990) "Psychotherapy for the treatment of depression: A comprehensive review of controlled outcome research", *Psychological Bulletin*, 108: 30–49.

Rogers, C. R. (1951) *Client-centered Therapy*. Boston: Houghton Mifflin.

Rogers, C. R. (1961) *On Becoming a Person*. Boston: Houghton Mifflin.

Sacks, O. (1998) *The Man Who Mistook His Wife for a Hat*. New York: Touchstone.

Saleebey, D. (1998) "Constructing the community: Emergent uses of social constructionism in economically distressed communities", in C. Franklin and P. S. Nurius (eds), *Constructivism in Practice*, pp. 291–310. Milwaukee, WI: Families International.

Seikkula, J., Alakare, B. and Aaltonen, J. (2001a) "Open dialogue in psychosis I: An introduction and case illustration", *Journal of Constructivist Psychology*, 14: 247–266.

Seikkula, J., Alakare, B. and Aaltonen, J. (2001b) "Open dialogue in psychosis II: A comparison of good and poor outcome cases", *Journal of Constructivist Psychology*, 14: 267–283.

Sewell, K. W., Baldwin, C. L. and Moes, A. J. (1998) "The multiple self awareness group", *Journal of Constructivist Psychology*, 11: 59–78.

Spence, D. (1982) *Narrative and Historical Truth*. New York: Norton.

Vaihinger, H. (1924) *The Philosophy of "As If"*. Berlin, Germany: Reuther & Reichard.

Vasco, A. B. (1994) "Correlates of constructivism among Portuguese therapists", *Journal of Constructivist Psychology*, 7: 1–16.

Vincent, N. and LeBow, M. (1995) "Treatment preference and acceptability: Epistemology and locus of control", *Journal of Constructivist Psychotherapy*, 8: 81–96.

Viney, L. L. (1988) "Which data-collection methods are appropriate for a constructivist psychology?" *International Journal of Personal Construct Psychology*, 1: 191–203.

Viney, L. L., Metcalfe, C. and Winter, D. A. (2005) "The effectiveness of personal construct psychotherapy: A meta-analysis", in D. Winter and L. Viney (eds), *Personal Construct Psychotherapy: Advances in Theory, Practice, and Research*, pp. 347–364. London: Whurr.

Wachtel, P. (1991) "From eclecticism to synthesis: Toward a more seamless psychotherapy integration", *Journal of Psychotherapy Integration*, 1: 43–54.

Weber, C., Bronner, E., Their, P., Kingreen, D. and Klapp, B. (2000) "Body construct systems of patients with hematological malignancies", in J. W. Scheer (ed.), *The Person in Society: Challenges to a Constructivist Theory*, pp. 328–339. Giessen, Germany: Psychosozial Verlag.

Whitaker, C. A. and Keith, D. V. (1981) "Symbolic-experiential family therapy", in A. S. Gurman and D. P. Kniskern (eds), *Handbook of Family Therapy*, pp. 187–225. New York: Brunner Mazel.

White, M. and Epston, D. (1990) *Narrative Means to Therapeutic Ends*. New York: Norton.

Williams, A. M., Diehl, N. S. and Mahoney, M. J. (2002) "Mirrortime: Empirical findings and implications for a constructivist psychotherapeutic technique", *Journal of Constructivist Psychology*, 15: 21–40.

Winslade, J. and Monk, G. (2001) *Narrative Mediation*. San Francisco: Jossey-Bass.

Winter, D. A. (1990) "Therapeutic alternatives for psychological disorder", in G. J. Neimeyer and R. A. Neimeyer (eds), *Advances in Personal Construct Psychology*, Vol. 1, pp. 89–116. Greenwich, CT: JAI.

Winter, D. A. (1992) *Personal Construct Psychology in Clinical Practice*. London: Routledge.

Winter, D. A. and Watson, S. (1999) "Personal construct theory and the cognitive therapies: Different in theory but can they be differentiated in practice?" *Journal of Constructivist Psychology*, 12: 1–22.

# Index